Berlin: A Spy's Guide to its Cold War History in Story and Image

by James Stejskal

Issued in print and electronic formats.

ISBN: 978-1-998501-64-9 (hardcover)
ISBN: 978-1-998501-60-1 (paperback)
ISBN: 978-1-998501-61-8 (ebook)

Cover & Interior Design: Axel Peralta

Double Dagger Books
Toronto, Ontario, Canada
www.doubledagger.ca

Contents

Introduction

This book is about the history of Cold War Berlin and about espionage. The two were inseparable for nearly a generation. Here are some of the stories of spies and spy masters told from the perspective of someone who lived and worked there during 10 years of the Cold War.

In February 1977, I boarded a Pan Am flight from JFK Airport to Frankfurt and then onward to Berlin. At Tegel Airport I met a comrade I knew from a previous stateside assignment and after throwing my bags in the VW Bus, we drove to the American sector in the southern part of the city. There I met the team I would be working with for the next four years. Although I had traveled outside the United States before, this would be my first long-term assignment overseas and it would be a formative time in my life. Just 23 years old, I'd never lived in such a large and diverse city as Berlin. Then and as it had always been, Berlin was one of the most edgy cities in Europe, let alone Germany. In the 1920s and early 1930s, it was the center of the Avant-Garde movement and home to a very free-thinking populace, which was probably why Adolf Hitler considered it "degenerate."

During the Cold War, Berlin was actually two cities. West Berlin was modern, dynamic, and free but enclosed like a cage by the "Anti-fascist Protection Barrier" aka the Wall. East Berlin was a stagnant controlled, police state with a population that silently endured rather than fought its oppression.

I remember walking along Bernauer Straße next to the Wall in the early evening fog, S-Bahn trains rattling along on the overhead tracks nearby. You could easily think you were taking part in a movie like *The Third Man or The Spy Who Came in From the Cold*. Not 10 meters away was the front line of an existential struggle between two cultures that stood ready to go to war. The front line encircled you, your home, your family—everything—there was no rear area for a safe retreat. You lived deep inside what was already enemy territory. Yet across the street you could walk into a *Kneipe* and order a beer and schnitzel and sit quietly reading a book, completely oblivious to a conflict that was waiting to happen. You were not reading about history, you were living in the middle of it.

The history of Berlin weighed down oppressively at times. A sign on a building facade commemorated the events of *Kristallnacht*, the night of broken glass when the anti-Jewish pogroms started in 1938. The march of jackboots through the narrow streets echoed in not-so-distant memories. To escape, there were the beaches of the Wannsee where many came to forget that they were locked inside a huge cage. Spring and summer seemed to signal both renewal and survival.

For me, Berlin was the perfect place to learn a trade.

I came to the world of intelligence operations and espionage in a convoluted way. My first job was working in a car wash during high school. After that, I bounced around a bit. I became a swimming instructor, a SCUBA diver, and I drove trucks for a construction company. I tried college, but ended up in the military and trained to become a paratrooper. One thing led to another and I ended up in the U.S. Army Special Forces and was involved in special ops and intelligence work. When I finally retired from the military after 23 years, I was recruited by an organization I'll just call the "agency." With both organizations, I traveled around the world conducting operations in the gray and black areas of international relations. The things I describe in this book are a result of those experiences, the people I worked with or against, and the stories I heard. The book is not about me; it is about the craft of intelligence and the people who practiced it in the city of Berlin at the very center of the Cold War.

The title "City of Spies" has been claimed by many cities, some deservedly, some perhaps because of their exotic locations. Vienna, London, Washington D.C., and Moscow have all had their share of "spy incidents." Shanghai and Istanbul also, because they are so unique in history, culture, and their proximity to regional hot spots make them exotic and often dangerous spy cities. But we also can't forget places like Stockholm, Havana, Islamabad, or even Miami.

So many of those locations have some claim to the title, but only one has, in my view at least, the best claim to be known as "The City of Spies" and that is Berlin. A city that first played a central role in the world wars of the 20th Century and then as a city occupied by four foreign powers. The USA, USSR, UK, and France were once allied in the great crusade of WWII, but when the war ended in 1945, they became enemies: the Warsaw Pact vs. NATO. During the Cold War, Berlin was probably the most active of all the spy havens on Earth. Its central European location and its unusual status on the world stage made it a focal point for intelligence operations.

From 1945 to 1990, the intelligence and security services of the four occupying powers as well as those of the German Democratic Republic (East Germany) and the Federal Republic of Germany (West Germany) played an intricate and often deadly game of cat and mouse on the streets of an occupied and divided Berlin.[1] But many other countries' intelligence services as well as rebel expatriate and revolutionary organizations like the Red Army Faction (RAF), the Palestinian Liberation Organization (PLO) and the Democratic Party of Iranian Kurdistan (PDKI) operated in the city.

It is the history and very unique atmosphere of Berlin that makes it one of my favorite places. When I was posted there in the late 1970s and through the 1980s up until the Berlin Wall came down in 1989, I experienced what those often very tense years were like. When Germany reunified, Berlin's special place in espionage operations was diminished, but it did not disappear. There are still more spies in Berlin than any other city on this planet. Yes, there are other focal points for intelligence operatives these days, but Berlin remains the premier Spy City.

Here then, is my compilation in photos and words of the "Who, What, Where, Why, and How" that made Berlin the "City of Spies."

---

[1] The Federal Republic of Germany (West Germany) was not permitted to send its military or security services into the city of Berlin by treaty. The Democratic Republic of Germany (East Germany) ignored those restrictions.

Glossary of Abbreviations and Terms

AGM/S - Arbeitsgruppe des Ministers / Sonderaufgaben - Minister's Working Group / Special Tasks (GDR)

Bahnhof - Station

BA or **BArch** - Bundesarchiv / Federal Archive (FRG)

BOB - Berlin Operations Base (CIA)

BND - *Bundesnachrichtendienst* / Federal Intelligence Service (FRG)

BRIXMIS - British Commanders'-in-Chief Mission to the Soviet Forces in Germany

BRD - *Bundes Republik Deutschland* (West Germany) also FRG

BfV - *Bundesamt für Verfassungsschutz* / Federal Office for the Protection of the Constitution (FRG)

BStU - Bundesbeauftragter für die Stasi-Unterlagen / Stasi Records Agency (FRG)

BW - *Bundeswehr* (BW) / Armed Forces (FRG)

CD - Concealment Device

CIA - Central Intelligence Agency (USA)

CPU - Car Pick-up

CO - Case Officer (UK / USA), may also be referred to as an Agent Handler or Operations Officer

Code Word - Highly classified, compartmented information

CT - Counter-terrorism

DD / DLD - Dead Drop, Dead Letter Drop

DDR - *Deutsche Demokratische Republik* (East Germany) also GDR

Det "A" - Detachment "A" / 39th Special Forces Detachment Berlin (USA)

DGSE - *Sécurité extérieure* / External Security Service - succeeded the SDECE in 1982 (France)

FO - *Führungsoffizier* / Agent Handler (GDR)

Four Powers - USA, UK, USSR, and France

FRG - Federal Republic of Germany (West Germany) also BRD

Führungsoffizier - Case Officer (GDR/FRG)

GCHQ - Government Communications Headquarters (UK)

GDR - German Democratic Republic (East Germany) also GDR

GHI - *Geheimer Hauptinformator* / Secret main informant (GDR)

GM - *Geheime Mitarbeiter* / Secret Collaborator (GDR)

GRU - *Glavnoye razvedyvatel'noye upravleniye* / Military Main Intelligence Directorate (USSR)

GSFG - Group of Soviet Forces in Germany (USSR)

GT - *Grenztruppen* / Border Troops (GDR)

HVA - *Hauptverwaltung Aufklärung* / Main Directorate for Reconnaissance (GDR)

IM - *Inoffizieller Mitarbeiter* (GDR)

IMA - *Inoffizieller Mitarbeiter mit besonderen Aufgaben* / Unofficial collaborator with special tasks (GDR)

IMB - *Inoffizieller Mitarbeiter der Abwehr mit Feindverbindung* / Unofficial collaborator with enemy-connections (GDR)

IO - Intelligence Officer

JAROC (B) - Joint Allied Refugee Operations Center, Berlin (US)

KGB - *Komitet gosudarstvennoy bezopasnosti* / Committee for State Security (USSR) preceded by the MGB.

MGB - *Ministerstvo gosudarstvennoy bezopasnosti* / Ministry for State Security (USSR), KGB predecessor.

MAD - *Militärische Abschirmdienst* / Ministry of Defense Counter-intelligence Service (FRG)

MfS - *Ministerium für Staatssicherheit - "Stasi"* / Ministry for State Security (GDR)

MI - Military Intelligence (USA / UK)

MICE - the motivations for spying: Money, Ideology, Compromise, Ego

MLM - Military Liaison Mission (US, UK, FR, USSR)

MO - Modus Operandi / method of operation

Mole - a spy recruited by the opposition inside an intelligence organization. A double agent, a traitor.

MVM - *Militärische Verbindungsmission* or Military Liaison Mission (MLM)

NARA - National Archives and Records Administration (USA)

NATO - North Atlantic Treaty Organization

NAZI - *Nationalsozialist* from NSDAP or National Socialist Workers Party (3rd Reich Germany)

NKVD - Predecessor of the KGB (USSR)

NVA - *Nationale Volksarmee* / National People's Army (GDR)

NSA - National Security Agency (USA)

NSDAP - *Nationalsozialistische Deutsche Arbeiterpartei* / National Socialist German Workers Party or Nazi

NTC - non-technical communications

OibE - *Offizier im besonderen Einsatz* / Officer on Special Duty (GDR)

PM - Personal Meet

PSSE-B - Physical Security Support Element Berlin / 410th Special Forces Detachment Berlin

RAF - *Rote Armee Faktion* / Red Army Faction

Rezidentura - Russian or Soviet intelligence station inside an embassy overseas. (USSR)

SANER - Memory aid for a communications plan: Scheduled, Alternate, Non-scheduled, Emergency, Reserve

SDECE (DGSE after 1982) - Sécurité extérieure / External Security Service (France)

SDR - Surveillance Detection Route

SED - *Sozialistische Einheitspartei Deutschland* / Socialist Unity Party Germany (GDR communist party)

SF - Special Forces (USA/UK)

SIS (MI-6) - Secret Intelligence Service (UK)

SM - Social Media

Spetsnaz - *Voyska spetsialnogo naznacheniya* / Special Purpose Forces (USSR)

SS - Signal Site

Stasi - *Staatssicherheit* / State Security, see MfS

SVR - *Sluzhba vneshney razvedki Rossiyskoy Federatsii* / Foreign Intelligence Service of the Russian Federation. Successor to the KGB. (Russia)

USMLM - U.S. Military Liaison Mission to the Soviet Forces in Germany (USA)

USSR - Union of Soviet Socialist Republics (now Russia)

Vopo - *Volkspolizei* / People's Police (GDR)

Westarbeit - Foreign intelligence operations against western countries (GDR)

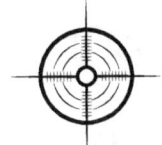

CHAPTER I
Berlin's Special History

Berlin. A city that has always been a playground for spies, intelligence officers, and their masters. Throw in an occasional anarchist, terrorist, or freedom fighter (depending on which side of the definition you're viewing them from) and you have a cauldron of intrigue, blackmail, subterfuge, and deception. Even before World War II, Berlin was a focal point of espionage, as German Chancellor Otto von Bismarck set up an intelligence network in Berlin that worked very successfully against his rivals and enemies across Europe. Names like Baron August Schluga von Rastenfeld and Wilhelm Johann Carl Eduard Stiebe are cited among the inventors of modern "intelligence collection."[2]

The one event that sealed its preeminent status as the "City of Spies" was Hitler's failed attempt to bring Europe under the Third Reich's control. At the end of World War II, Germany and Berlin were occupied by the victors and became the focal point of espionage during the Cold War.

Both sides, the Soviets and their Warsaw Pact allies on one, and the U.S. and their NATO allies on the other, used Berlin as jumping off point for operations. The West, however, used their presence in Berlin to be a thorn in the side of the communists as an "Outpost of Freedom," a listening post, a haven in the middle of Eastern Europe, and simply as a symbol of resolve.

The West German politician and Mayor of Berlin, Willi Brandt, put it best:

"The task of West Berlin is to make the stabilization of the GDR as difficult as possible, to slow it down as much as possible."

In Europe, Berlin is a relatively young city. Its name is just over 750 years old but it has seen more than its share of cultural, military, and political history. In 1990, when the Wall fell and Berlin again became the capital of a re-unified Germany, many of the "Spy Game" players came off the board. No more East German Ministry for State Security (Stasi) officers and agents roamed the streets. The Soviets (now Russians once again) lost their huge fiefdom at Karlshorst-Berlin and with it their advantage of having both KGB and GRU offices in the country. Many terrorists also lost their safe havens.

That said, Berlin is still at the center of Europe's international relations. A crossroads for war and espionage, Berlin's status and history ensured it would remain a Spy Capital following World War II, through the Cold War, and even into our present day.

---

[2] I imagine that Moses would be considered the first spy chief, followed by many nameless (as they should be) individuals and the more well known like Queen Elizabeth's own Sir Francis Walsingham. In the United States, General George Washington was the 1st spy chief.

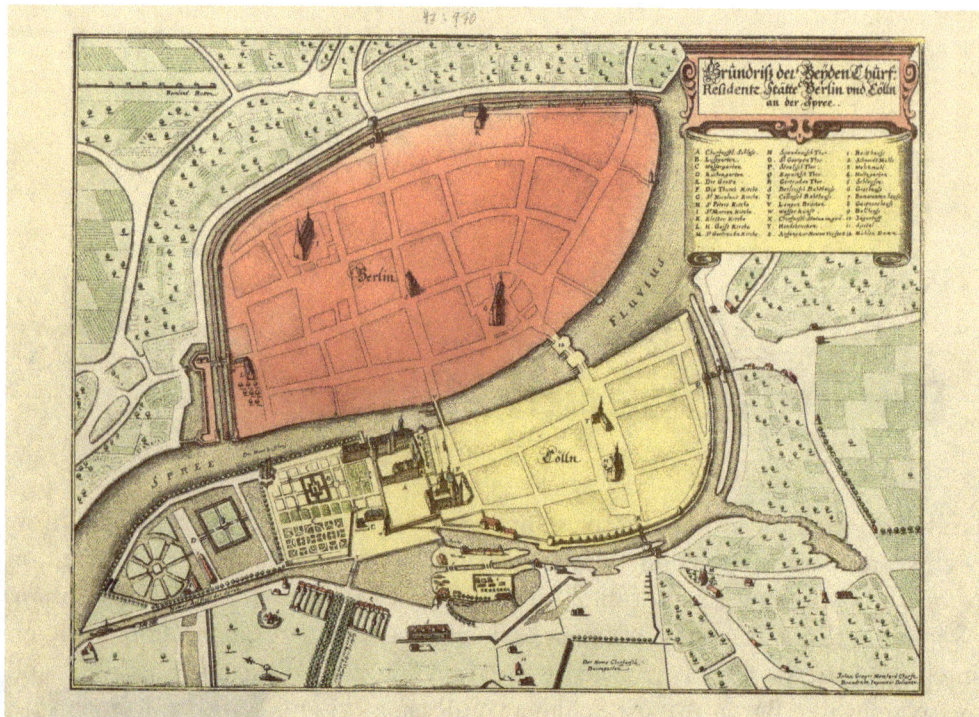

Oldest known Map of Berlin (Credit: Memhardt, Johann Gregor. *"Grundriss Der Beyden Churf. Residentz Stätte Berlin Und Cölln an Der Spree"* - 1652. PD)

Occupation zones - slicing up the city

Months before the end of the war, the United States, the Soviet Union, and the United Kingdom (wartime allies), met at Yalta (in Crimea) to decide Germany's post-war fate. There, Josef Stalin, Franklin D. Roosevelt, and Winston Churchill decided to divide Germany into four occupation zones. France was still under German occupation but the presumption was that a liberated France would be the fourth partner.

What remained of pre-war Germany west of the Oder-Neisse line was divided into four occupation zones, each controlled by one of the four occupying Allied nations, aka the Four Powers: the United States, the United Kingdom, France and the Soviet Union. Berlin, the former capital, became the seat of the Allied Control Council and was similarly subdivided into four sectors. Despite the city's location, 110 kilometers distant from the frontier of what would become the two Germanys, and well inside the Soviet zone, the Western Allies were determined to hold onto Berlin, much to the annoyance of the Soviets and the communist East Germans.

The eastern city districts of Mitte, Prenzlauer Berg, Friedrichshain, Pankow, Weißensee, Lichtenberg, Treptow and Köpenick formed the Soviet sector of Greater Berlin and a separate city government.[3]

In the western sector, the districts of Reinickendorf, Spandau, Wedding, Charlottenburg, Tiergarten, Kreuzberg, Schöneberg, Wilmersdorf, Tempelhof, Zehlendorf, Steglitz, and Neukölln became West Berlin.

Only a year later in March 1946, Churchill delivered his famous speech that declared an "Iron Curtain" had fallen across Eastern Europe. The former Allies' wartime relations began to take a chilly turn and the Cold War would soon dominate European affairs for the next 45 years.

---

[3] In 1949, East Berlin became the capital of the German Democratic Republic (GDR), while West Germany (FRG) made its capital in Bonn.

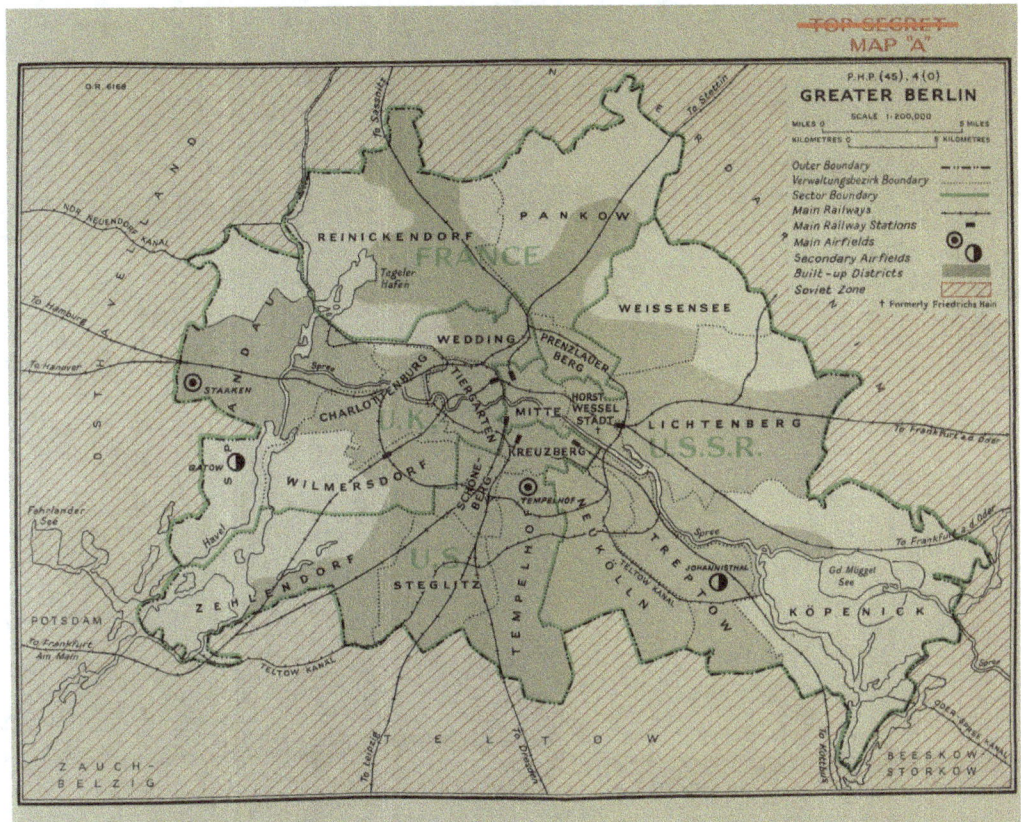

UK Foreign Office map showing occupation of Berlin in 1948. (Credit: FO371.50831)

After the war, neither the United States or the United Kingdom fully appreciated the fault line created with a defeated and divided Germany as the Soviet Union became ever more hostile in its ideology and oppression in Eastern Europe.

There were two different solutions. Realizing that the USSR was no longer an ally, the West was determined to make Germany a bulwark against communism and implemented the Marshall Plan with nearly 1.5 billion dollars worth of aid poured into West Germany.

The Soviet Union was primarily interested in how they could use Germany's enormous geopolitical and economic weight in their favor. Needing resources, Moscow ordered that everything useful, nailed down or otherwise, should be taken back to the motherland as war reparations. East Germany ended up stripped of its economic potential while the West experienced an economic miracle.

The military occupation was very different on each side of the frontier as well. In the West there were (mostly) well-disciplined soldiers who were initially regarded as enemies and later as guardians. In the East, the Soviets exacted retribution against the civilian populace for what Hitler's armies had perpetrated on the Eastern Front.

In the East, the newly established communist *Sozialistische Einheitspartei Deutschland* or Socialist Unity Party Germany (which never permitted a popular vote) quickly installed an all-pervasive internal security system that guaranteed its dominance and survival.[4] The suppression of the 1953 workers uprising — crushed by the Red Army — only proved to the populace that they had given up one dictatorship for another.

---

[4] The Ministry for State Security's motto "Sword and Shield of the Party" was an indicator of its true allegiance.

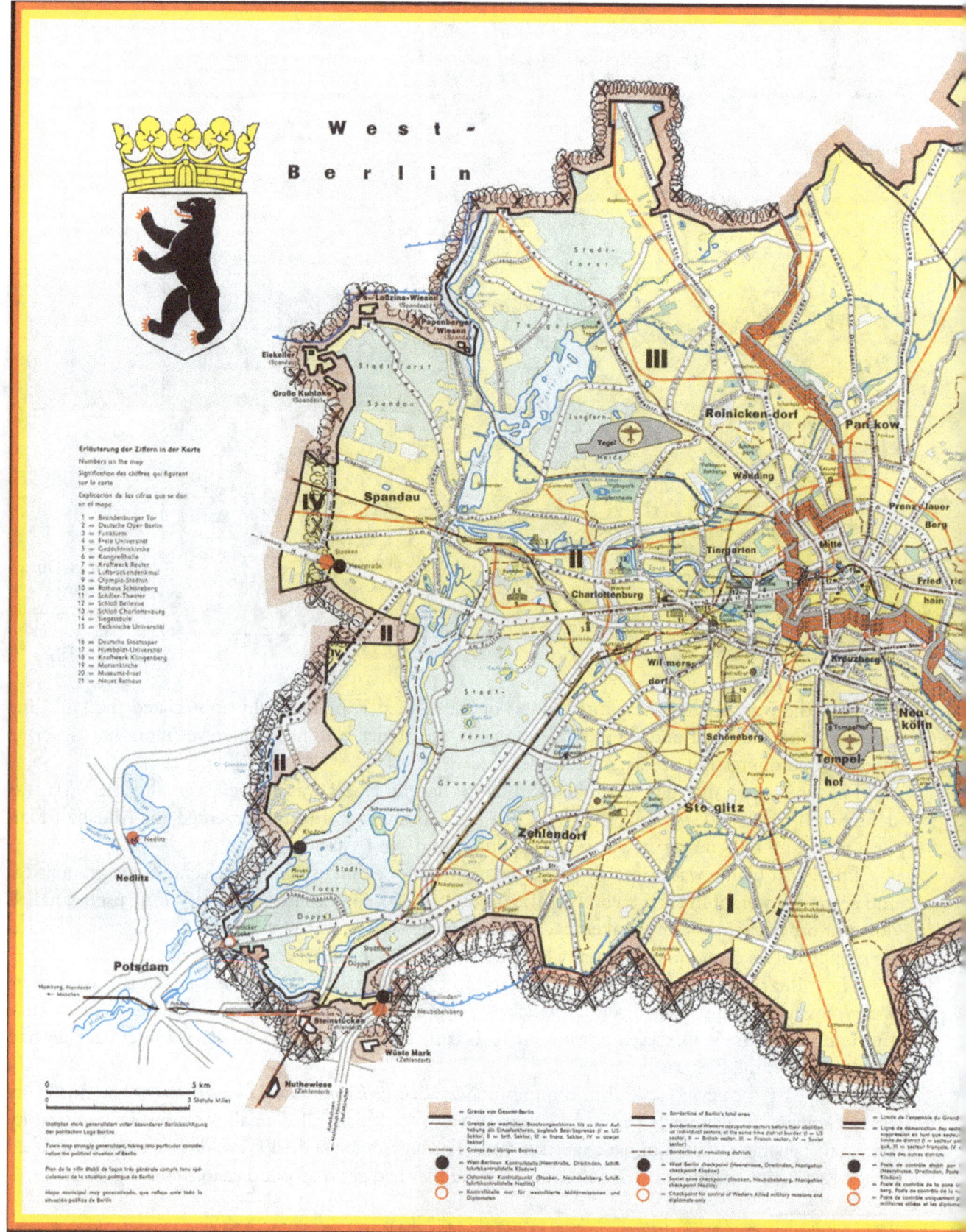

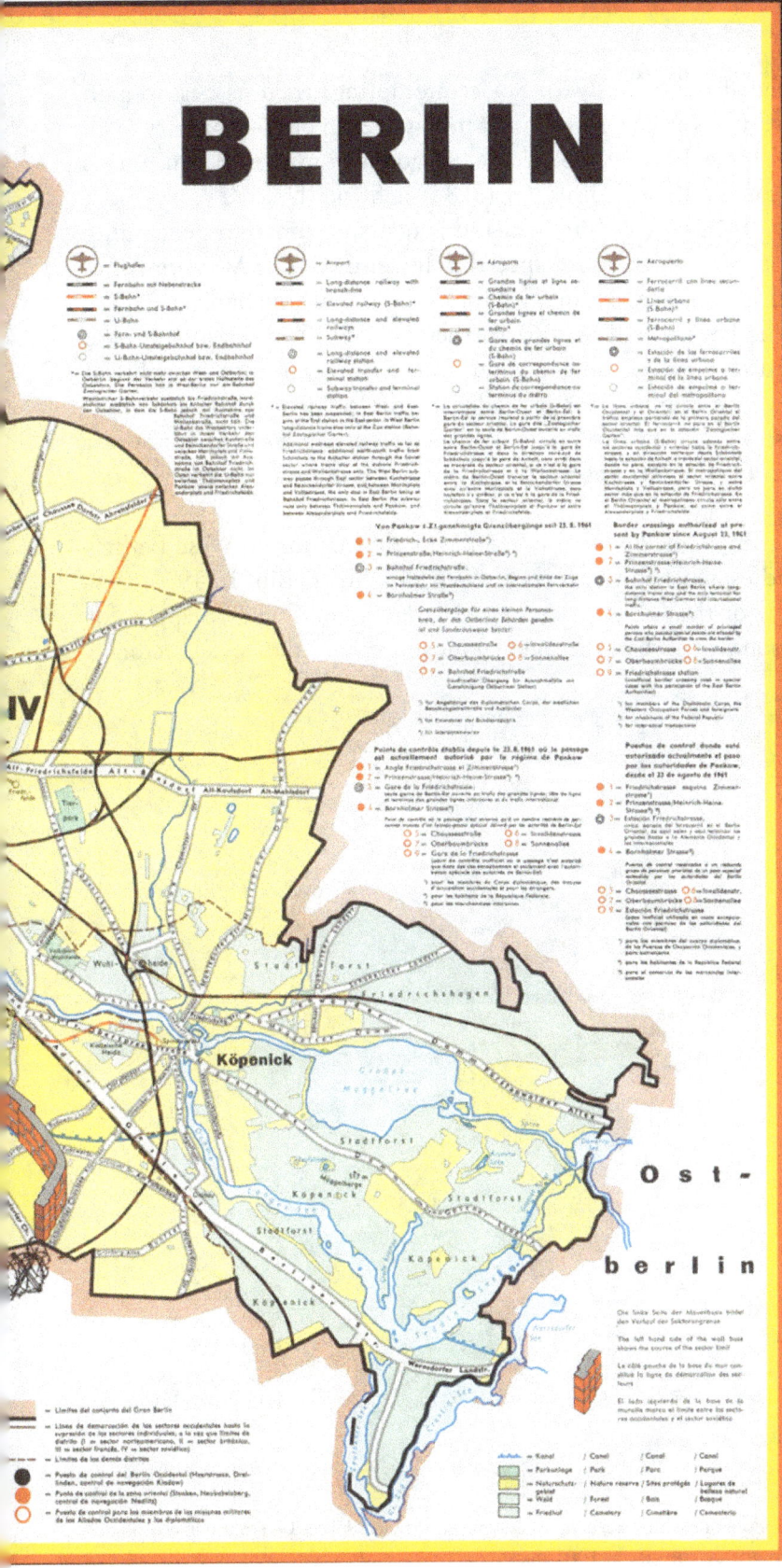

Cold War Berlin 1963 Map. (credit:
- Presse- und Informationsamt des
Landes Berlin)

From the beginning, the government of the GDR (with Soviet prompting) tried its best to gain control of the entire city, not only because it was seat of government in East Berlin but — contrary to all agreements — it proclaimed Berlin as its capital. In 1949, it blockaded all goods from West Berlin, a crisis that was overcome with Allied resolve and the Berlin Airlift. In 1958, the Soviet Union's party leader Khrushchev again contested the validity of the London Protocol and issued an ultimatum demanding that West Berlin be converted into a free city as a so-called special political unit. The Western Allies rejected the Soviet Union's demands and the status quo remained for the most part unchanged.

The East German construction of the Berlin Wall in 1961 further isolated West Berlin from the East as the GDR government continued to push measures to integrate East Berlin into its political sphere. In January 1962, NVA military conscription was extended to the residents of East Berlin. (West Berlin remained a haven for those who wished to dodge the West German *Bundeswehr's* draft until 1990), The Soviet city command in East Berlin was dissolved and replaced by a city commander of the National People's Army (NVA).[5]

The Four Power Agreement on Berlin, signed in 1971, regulated the nature of West Berlin's connections to the Federal Republic and established the special status of all of Berlin. In 1976, East Berlin was officially declared the capital of the GDR. Allied special rights continued to apply, for example, uniformed Allied military personnel still had the right to move freely in the Soviet sector.

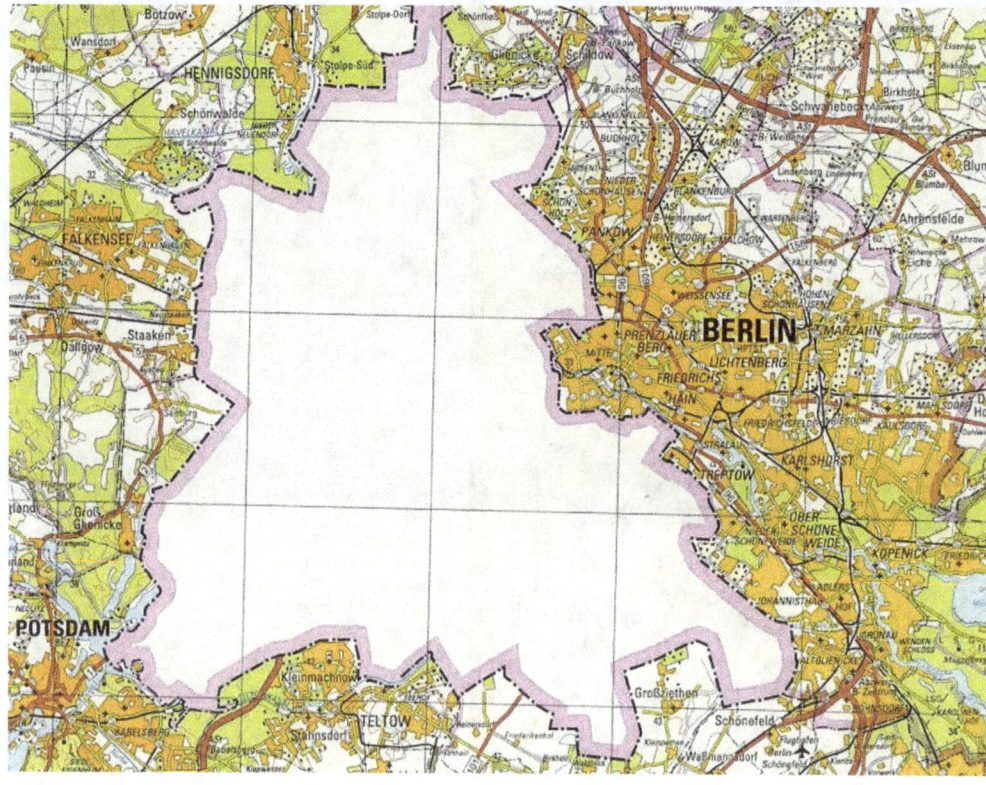

How the East Germans saw West Berlin (credit: RV Reise & Verkehrverlag, Ed.14, 1988/1989)

---

[5] This was purely for show as the USSR maintained its headquarters for the Group of Soviet Forces Germany just outside the city and it had another military headquarters inside the city at Karlshorst.

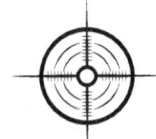

CHAPTER II
The Cold War Players in Berlin

The Occupation Forces

Although Berlin was off limits to German army forces, the West German *Bundeswehr* (BW) and the East German *Nationale Volksarmee* (NVA) largely ignored the rules. The Soviet Army had a huge presence in the country and in the city with its headquarters located at Zossen, GDR and the 8th Guards Army at Weimer-Nohra outside the city. The Soviet Group of Soviet Forces Germany (GSFG) numbered approximately 380,000 combat ready troops organized into 20 ground force divisions and one air army, while its Warsaw Pact ally, the East German National People's Army (NVA) numbered between 180,000 (peacetime) and 350,000 (wartime-footing) troops spread across ten combat ready divisions.

The Allied occupation forces of Berlin were present in far fewer numbers as Berlin was regarded more as showplace, an "Outpost of Freedom" deep inside East Germany, than a strong point to be defended in case of war. The American, British, and French military forces in Berlin numbered around 12,000 in total. All foreign military forces were removed from a reunited Berlin by 1994.

CIA / Berlin Operations Base (BOB)

BOB was the headquarters of the Central Intelligence Agency (CIA) and its predecessor, the Office of Strategic Services, in West Berlin during the Cold War. Established by the OSS on 4 July 1945, it was originally located in a villa at 19-21 Föhrenweg in the suburb of Dahlem in the Zehlendorf district, an area which had suffered minimal bomb damage in World War II. By the early 1950s the base moved from the Föhrenweg villa to the more secure U.S. Armed Forces Berlin Headquarters compound located on Clayallee where it was located in Building 6A.

During its early years, BOB vied for primacy with CIA's operating base in Vienna. When the Allied occupation of Austria ended and Vienna ceased to be a Four Power territory, BOB became the forefront of US intelligence during the Cold War.

Initially, there was little focus on the Soviets as they were considered allies. Slowly, as Stalin's intentions were discerned, operations were mostly directed at the threat of war and the immediate concerns about what Soviet forces were doing. Much of BOB's efforts were directed to war planning and stay-behind activities in the event of a military confrontation. Only in the late 1950s when Soviet Premier Nikita Khrushchev threatened to abrogate existing treaties and sign a separate peace treaty with the East Germany were the CIA's efforts redirected at strategic collection against the Warsaw Pact countries.

BOB was deactivated in a ceremony held on 4 July 1994.

Föhrenweg offices of CIA / BOB , 2024 (credit: author)

Clay Compound Saargemunderstraße side gate, 2024 (credit: author)

Clay Compound Building 6 BOB/CIA - now Metro Gardens #25 (credit: author)

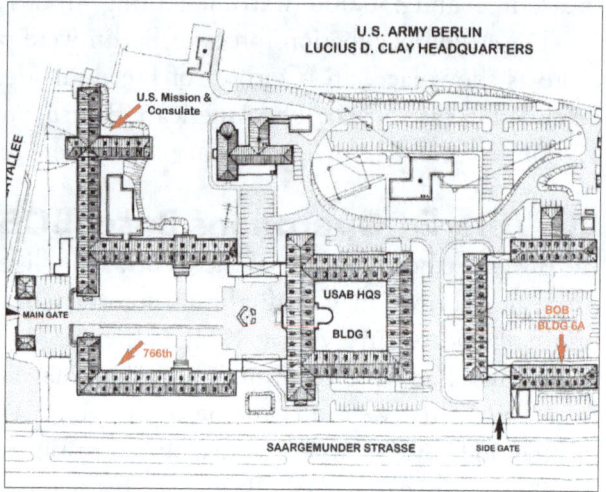

Clay Compound Map, 1985 (credit: U.S. Army)

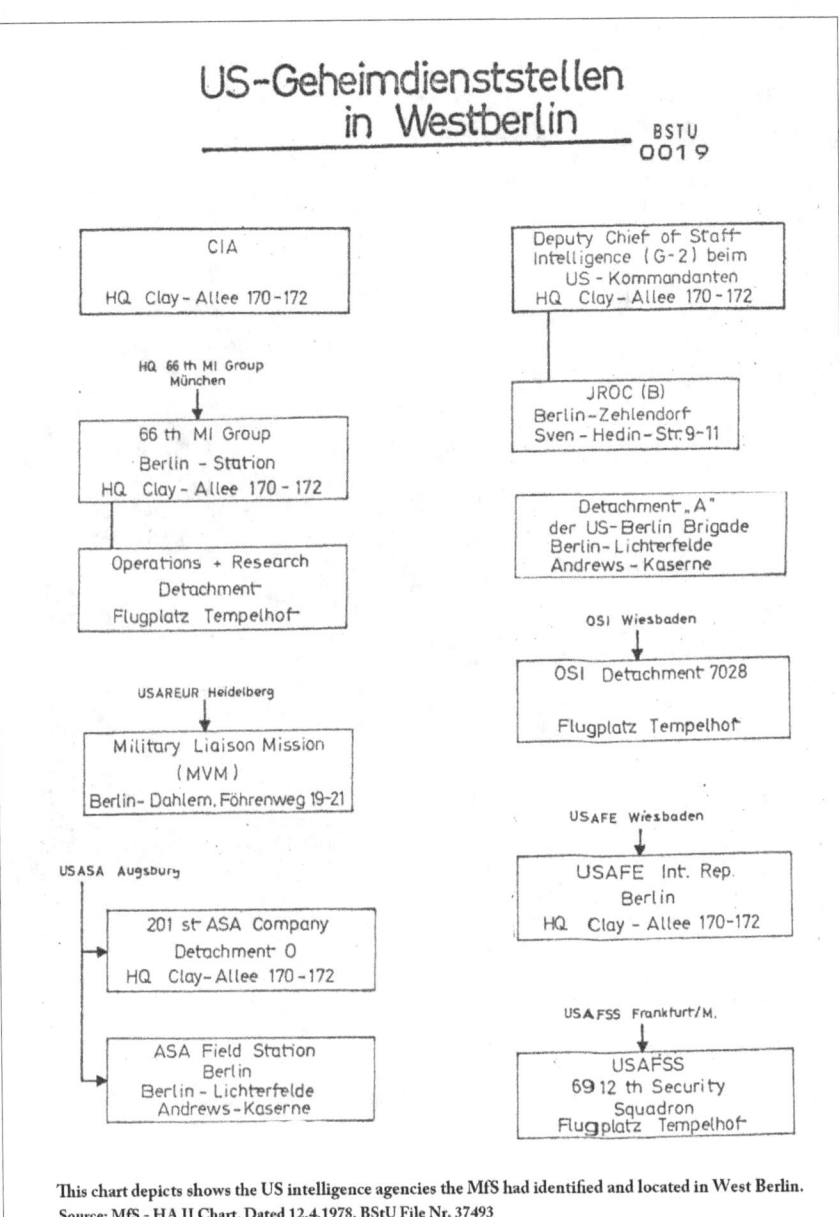

US-Geheimdienststellen in Westberlin

BSTU 0019

CIA HQ Clay-Allee 170-172	Deputy Chief of Staff Intelligence (G-2) beim US-Kommandanten HQ Clay-Allee 170-172

HQ 66th MI Group München

66th MI Group Berlin-Station HQ Clay-Allee 170-172	JROC (B) Berlin-Zehlendorf Sven-Hedin-Str. 9-11

Operations + Research Detachment Flugplatz Tempelhof	Detachment „A" der US-Berlin Brigade Berlin-Lichterfelde Andrews-Kaserne

USAREUR Heidelberg

OSI Wiesbaden

Military Liaison Mission (MVM) Berlin-Dahlem, Föhrenweg 19-21	OSI Detachment 7028 Flugplatz Tempelhof

USASA Augsburg

USAFE Wiesbaden

201st ASA Company Detachment 0 HQ Clay-Allee 170-172	USAFE Int. Rep. Berlin HQ Clay-Allee 170-172

USAFSS Frankfurt/M.

ASA Field Station Berlin Berlin-Lichterfelde Andrews-Kaserne	USAFSS 6912th Security Squadron Flugplatz Tempelhof

This chart depicts shows the US intelligence agencies the MfS had identified and located in West Berlin.
Source: MfS - HA II Chart, Dated 12.4.1978, BStU File Nr. 37493

Stasi Diagram of US Intelligence units in Berlin, 1978 (credit: BA-BStU)

766 Military Intelligence Detachment (MID)

The 766th MID was a subunit of the 66th Military Intelligence Group headquartered in Stuttgart, FRG with a mission to conduct counterintelligence. The 766th was responsible for Region VIII — the city of Berlin. Its offices were located in the U.S. Headquarters at Clay Compound.

From its establishment in Berlin in 1945 until it was closed down in 1994, the 766th occupied itself with protecting the operations and information of the Berlin Brigade from espionage operations. It had a number of successes, but there were also failures, some of which are detailed in the pages that follow.

Teufelsberg from the air circa 1985 (credit: U.S. Army)

Stasi Surveillance Photo of the Teufelsberg Site (credit: BStU, MfS, HA III, Nr. 14455, Bl. 105)

Teufelsberg currently serves as an artists' playground (credit: author)

National Security Agency — NSA

During the Cold War, the National Security Agency (NSA) was responsible for the U.S. Government efforts in signals intelligence (SIGINT), often with partners from the U.S. military and Allied partners, usually from the United Kingdom.

In Berlin, the NSA along with like military components maintained three listening sites that were used to collect signals intelligence (radio, telephone, and later, satellite communications from the Warsaw Pact. The Teufelsberg site in western Berlin's Grünewald Forest was part of NSA's collection network, which the US intelligence service used to keep an eye on Moscow. From 1957 to 1991, the NSA maintained a presence on Teufelsberg and eavesdropped on communications as far east as the Soviet border with Poland and as far south as Czechoslovakia's border with Hungary.

NSA's analog, the British Government Communications Headquarters (GCHQ) was also heavily involved with communications intercepts at the American collection sites in Berlin. For those reasons, the NSA's locations and its personnel were high priority collection and recruitment targets for the Soviet KGB and East German MfS. Two of those cases are told in this book's later chapters.

British Forces Hqs Berlin Alderhof Olympia Stadion - the SIS Offices were on the 3rd Floor, the BRIXMIS Offices were on the 4th, (credit: author)

Eagle - Adler Hof Olympia Stadion (credit: author)

British Secret Intelligence Service / Military Intelligence Section 6 — SIS / MI6

The Secret Intelligence Service's mission is to collect foreign intelligence regarding foreign countries intentions and threats to Britain's national interests and security, and to protect the country's economic well-being. SIS works within the Foreign, Commonwealth & Development Office and falls under the supervision of the Foreign Secretary.

In Berlin, it was initially headquartered at the Savoy Hotel until it moved to new offices on the 3rd floor of the Adlerplatz Headquarters of the British Military Governor on the grounds of the Olympic Stadium.[6]

It often worked jointly with the American CIA/BOB and information was shared on a continual, if controlled basis. In the 1950s, both services cooperated to construct an underground tunnel from the Western Sector of Berlin into the East in order to tap into the communications lines of the Soviet and East German forces. Although the tunnel's existence was compromised by George Blake, a SIS officer who had been recruited by the KGB, the final evaluation is that the information gained from the operation was extremely valuable.

— Adlerplatz, Olympiapark, S-Bahnhof Olympiastadion (S3, S9)

---

[6] In Mick Herron's Slough House precursor novel, *The Secret Hours,* his protagonist, Jackson Lamb, finds his "secret" office to be located in a less than respectable neighborhood near a cat-house full of boisterous women. I'm still trying to locate his office in Berlin; it may take a while.

French External Security — SDECE/DGSE

The Direction générale de la Sécurité extérieure (DGSE) traces its origin to its predecessor organization, the Service de Documentation Extérieure et de Contre-Espionnage, (SDECE) which was established in 1946. Its founding was driven by the need to disassociate from the wartime Bureau Central de Renseignements et d'Action (BCRA), which was closely linked to the Gaullist movement. SDECE was also known as "la piscine" or "the Pool" due to its location near a public swimming pool in Paris. Ostensibly answering to the Minister of Defense, it actually reported to the French President.

Formed in December 1945, SDECE brought together several separate intelligence agencies, including the *Deuxième Bureau,* aka *2e Bureau* and the BRCA *(Bureau central de renseignements et d'action).*

Much like the CIA and SIS, SDECE's attempts to penetrate Eastern Europe were a disaster in the 1950s. The agency was riddled with French communists who reported to Moscow and all agents parachuted into Eastern Europe were captured.

Mistrust of the United States and Britain led to poor relations with both the CIA and SIS until the 1970s and even then, close coordination was difficult. A Soviet spy ring called SAPPHIRE was operating within the SDECE and was uncovered by the CIA through a defector but French President Charles De Gaulle believed the claim was a CIA plot to disorganize the SDECE. All co-operation with the CIA was broken off. In 1982, the François Mitterrand socialist government reformed SDECE and renamed it DGSE.

SDECE/DGSE operations were run from its offices in Napoleon Barracks near the former Tegel Airport in northwestern Berlin.

Ministerium für Staatssicherheit (MfS) — Stasi

Answerable only to the *Sozialistische Einheitspartei Deutschland* (SED), the Ministry for State Security was its "shield and sword," mandated to secure the party's rule. The SED governed the GDR for 40 years without ever being legitimized in a democratic election and maintained its position of power by means of a huge security apparatus.

The Ministry for State Security, or *"Stasi"* was founded in 1950 and was the cornerstone of East Germany's security apparatus. Set up under the direct supervision of the Soviet KGB, it was a domestic secret police organization and a foreign intelligence agency. It had its own prisons, its own militia, and its activities were not monitored or restricted in any way.

With an estimated one MfS officer for every 180 persons in East Germany it was probably the largest security organizations per capita in the world. In 1989, there were 91,000 full-time employees working in a controlled informant network that included **one in every three citizens.** To say it was all-pervasive is an understatement.

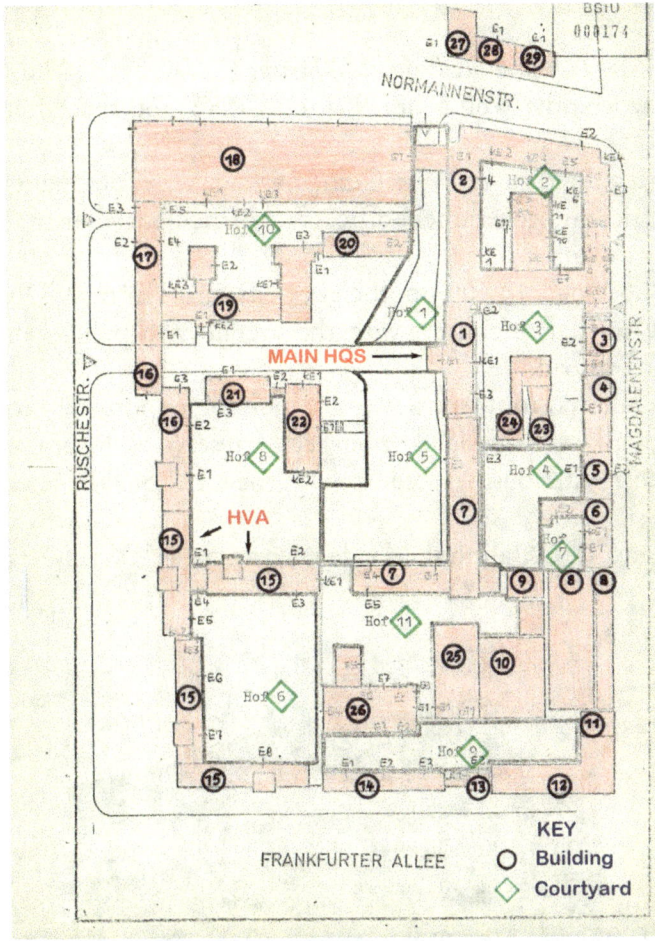

Diagram of MfS *"Stasi"* Central, Normannenstraße (credit: BStU)

If a person's ideas or attitudes deviated from the Party's norms, they were considered subversive and under the influence of "enemy headquarters" in the West. In order to control and eliminate "hostile negative elements," all areas of life of the population were targeted by *Stasi* surveillance.

The Ministry for State Security (MfS) was organized on military lines, and its structure was strictly centralized. From 1957 to 1989 it was headed by Erich Mielke, who had a decisive influence on its development.

Encouraged by their Soviet partners, the Ministry for State Security (MfS) acted with impunity and brutality during the early years of the GDR. Physical violence, arbitrary arrests, and kidnappings from West Berlin and West Germany were followed by show trials and often the imposition of draconian sentences including secret executions.

Although the passing of years tempered its actions somewhat, it never left them completely and its activities only nurtured popular dissatisfaction and opposition against the government. Those feeling led directly to the events of 1989 and dissolution of the German Democratic Republic.

Most of *Stasi's* internal security files survived and a mechanism to research the documents has been set up by the German Federal Archives.[7]

---

[7] Information can be found here: https://www.bundesarchiv.de/im-archiv-recherchieren/stasi-unterlagen-einsehen/

MfS HVA "Westarbeit"

Foreign espionage was the main responsibility of the *Hauptverwaltung Aufklärung* (HVA) or the Main Directorate for Reconnaissance. It was headed by Markus Wolf from 1952 until 1986, and thereafter by Werner Grossmann.

The HVA's espionage operations were largely directed at West Germany and West Berlin. Its agents infiltrated public institutions, political parties and government offices and carried out industrial and technical espionage against West German companies.

By 1989 the HVA had a full-time staff of 4,600, plus 13,400 unofficial collaborators in the GDR and another 1,500 in West Germany. The HVA acted in concert with the overall MfS policies of persecution within the GDR and in its operations abroad.

After the peaceful revolution the HVA was allowed to dissolve itself. It took the opportunity to destroy a large quantity of its documents but not all were shredded or burned. A reserve cache of the HVA's assets and agents managed to survive and mysteriously ended up with the CIA (See the later section on Rosewood / Rosenholz).

— *Stasimuseum*, Normannenstraße 20, Haus 1, U-Bahnhof Magdalenenstraße (U5), Bus via Frankfurter Allee (B1/B5)

MfS Chief Erich Mielke's Desk with Lenin Death Mask, 1990 (credit: author)

MfS Headquarters Haus 1 exterior (credit: author)

MfS Stasi" shield removed from Haus 1 (credit: author)

HVA "Spy Master" Markus Wolf, 1991 (credit: Roger Melis / author's collection)

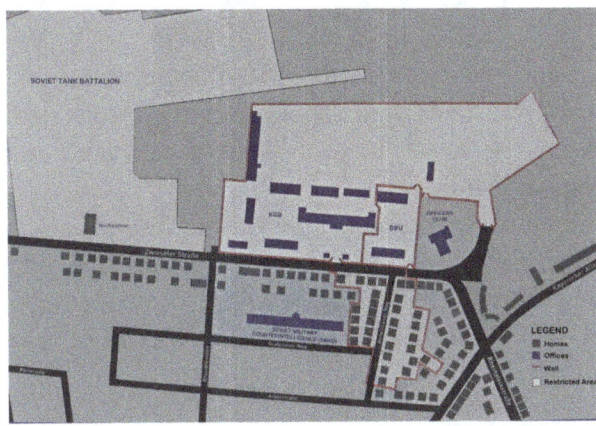

Map KGB / GRU Karlshorst Compound (author's collection)

Karlshorst - Site of the German Unconditional Surrender, 8 May 1945 (credit © Timofej Melnik / Museum Berlin-Karlshorst)

Soviet Security Poster — Iron Felix Dzierżyński, Creator of the Checka, KGB's predecessor - "Be watchful and vigilant!"

KGB / GRU

Tracing the activities of Soviet intelligence in Berlin following the war is difficult because there were many disparate organizations until the KGB (*Komitet gosudarstvennoy bezopasnosti* or Committee for State Security) was created in 1954. Once the KGB took primacy, it set up the largest and westernmost KGB office outside the Soviet Union in 1960.

The permanent location chosen was the former pioneer school of the German Wehrmacht.Berlin was of outstanding importance in the Cold War due to the presence of the Western Allies. Before that, the KGB had operated out of a smaller building in the Berlin-Karlshorst restricted area.

Around 500 to 1,300 KGB employees conducted espionage activities from Zwieseler Strasse into West Berlin and West Germany. Conversely, Karlshorst was also the focus of the Allied intel services, who saw the headquarters as a most important operational target.

Because of the paranoid nature of the Soviet secret services, the KGB and the Soviet military intelligence service, the GRU, distrusted each other. The GRU was located nearby but the two locations were separated by walls. The KGB's military counter-espionage was located in Potsdam's "Military Town No. 7."

While the GRU was (is) a military organization, it also conducted intelligence operations against civilian as well as military targets in West Berlin.

The Karlshorst location was also a center for repression and the securing of Soviet oppression.

In the struggle between East and West, no criticism or resistance from the population was tolerated. Many people were arrested and some were turned over to the Soviets in Karlshorst where there was a prison. Unlike the West, individual rights were not respected inside these walls.

In 1992, the property was handed over to the German government. Due to the site's historical status, some buildings remained standing after the withdrawal of the Russian forces in 1994 and several have been renovated as residential buildings. The Museum Berlin-Karlshorst is located nearby.

— Museum Berlin-Karlshorst, Zwieseler Straße 4, S-Bahnhof Karlshorst(S3) then Bus 296 to the Museum Karlshorst.

KGB Karlshorst
Main Building
(credit: author)

Karlshorst - Museum Berlin
(credit: author)

USMLM soldier observing Soviet troop train (credit: RH)

Military Liaison Missions - Legal Spying

The *Militärische Verbindungsmission* (MVM) or Military Liaison Missions (MLM) arose from reciprocal agreements formed immediately after the Second World War between the Western allied nations (U.S., UK, and France) and the USSR.

The British-Soviet liaison missions were the first to be established (September 1946) under the terms of the Robertson-Malinin Agreement (the respective commanders-in-chief). It also had the largest contingent of personnel with 31 accredited team members. Later agreements with the US (Huebner-Malinin, March 1947) and France (Noiret-Malinin, April 1947) permitted significantly fewer personnel, possibly because those Allied powers did not want large Soviet missions operating in their zones and vice versa.

Each Allied nations negotiated and signed its own agreement with Soviet Union but all permitted the deployment of small numbers of military intelligence personnel — together with associated support staff — in each other's occupation zone in Germany, ostensibly for the purposes of monitoring local events and furthering better relationships between the occupation forces, but in actuality they were collecting intelligence. The British, French and American missions matched the size of the counterpart Soviet missions into West Germany (the nominal post-war British, French and American zones of occupations).

The Allied MLM teams were based in West Berlin but started their "tours" from their respective national mission houses in Potsdam to the southwest of Berlin proper and across the Glieneke Bridge. The missions were in operation 24/7 throughout the Cold War period and only ended in 1990, just a few years prior to German reunification. The missions were named:
- British Commanders'-in-Chief Mission to the Soviet Forces in Germany (BRIXMIS)
- La Mission Militaire Francaise de Liaison (MMFL)
- U.S. Military Liaison Mission (USMLM)

Their reciprocal Soviet missions (SMLM) operated from Frankfurt am Main, Baden Baden, and Bünde, West Germany.

USMLM photograph of Soviet T-80 Tank under Tarp (credit: USMLM)

The three Allied missions covered the entire territory of the GDR with the objective of collecting intelligence information, overtly and covertly, that proved invaluable to their respective nations and to NATO. One of their most important activities was to photograph anything of interest, often from the inside of their cars as they drove. These missions — called "tours" — were conducted with an officer and one or two non-commissioned officers.[8]

"On every single day throughout the Cold War, eight or more Allied tours were roaming the countryside of East Germany. Every day, all night, each tour looking exactly for signs of imminence of hostilities or gathering intelligence."[9]

Eighty percent of East Germany was designated as permanent or temporary restricted areas (PRA/ TRA) that were off-limits to the Missions, but the teams would often secretly enter the zones, because that's where they expected the most valuable intelligence to be found.

Additionally, they would enter training areas and break into buildings or vehicles to take photographs of their opponent's equipment and documents. Much of the Soviet equipment would be moved by train or truck covered by tarps, requiring unique methods to photograph the equipment. Allied Special Forces operators would often ride along as part of the mission to collect information on potential wartime targets. They were fully trained to conduct the MLM mission tasks as well.

Soviet and East German military forces and Stasi cars would obstruct the Missions' activity by harassing, detaining and even ramming their cars off the road. Two Mission officers, one French (Philippe Mariotti) and one American, (Arthur D. Nicholson), were killed conducting these operations and a number of personnel were injured through the years.[10]

---

[8] Soviet *Spetsnaz* troops would have conducted similar tasks in West Germany with their SMLM tours.

[9] Colonel Roland Lajoie, Commander, USMLM.

[10] On March 22, 1984, a member of the French Mission lost his life in a staged traffic "accident." Almost exactly one year later, on March 24, 1985, Major Nicholson was shot and killed by a Soviet sentry.

BRIXMIS Haus
Potsdam (credit: PD)

BRIXMIS Car at speed
(credit: BRIXMIS / Military
Intelligence Museum)

In the estimation of each respective country's defense ministries, the Allied missions were the most prolific and useful collectors of military intelligence inside East Germany. It is believed, however, that the Soviet missions in West Germany were more oriented on clandestine collection operating bases from which intelligence agents could be run and supplied.[11]

— **MLM Headquarters locations in Berlin:**

USMLM Hqs, Dahlem, Föhrenweg 19-21 (See the CIA / BOB section above),

BRIXMIS Hqs, 4th floor, Adlerplatz, S-Bahnhof Olympiastadion (See SIS / MI6 above),

MLM Hqs, Napoleon Barracks, Tegel, Kurt-Schumacher-Damm (now Julius Leber Kaserne - home to the *Bundeswehr Wachbattalion),*

— **Potsdam Mission Houses:**

USMLM House (Sigismund Villa), Straße Am Lehnitzsee 8, Potsdam.

UK BRIXMIS House (Villa Metz), Seestrasse 34, Potsdam.

French MLM House (Villa Rumpf) / Seestraße 41, Potsdam.

Potsdam is best visited for a full day and should include the city's Prussian historical sites such as the Emperor Frederick the Great's Sanssouci Palace (built 1745-1747).

S-Bahn Hauptbahnhof Potsdam (S7).

---

[11] Aden C. Magee, The Cold War Wilderness of Mirrors: Counterintelligence and the U.S. and Soviet Military Liaison Missions 1947-1990, Casemate: Havertown, 2021.

DDR Paratrooper Photo
(author's collection)

And then there were the special folks...

MfS - AGM/S

Much like the USSR, the GDR decided it needed special operations forces for a possible conflict with Western Europe and NATO. Illegals were trained and placed in West Germany and other troops were prepared for combat at locations in East Germany. One of the primary training locations was at Hoppegarten just outside Berlin.

Several special sections were formed but the overarching organization responsible was the Minister's Working Group / Special Tasks (AGM/S). Training of the unit dealt with the operational reconnaissance, recruitment and control in the operational areas of West Germany and West Berlin, including the reconnaissance of enemy persons and objects as well as sabotage.

The MfS formulated its objective clearly: the AGM/S was "to be ready to successfully carry out active actions against the enemy and its hinterland in order to protect the German Democratic Republic."

The focus of the actions to be carried out was on specific enemy targets, including the armaments industry, telecommunications, energy supply, transport and water supply. The measures were intended to be suitable for hindering the enemy's preparations for war or, in the event of armed conflict, to impair its combat power.

Stasi's XXII
Counter-terror force
Training (credit:
BStU, HAXXII,
Fo, Nr. 21, Bild 3)

As early as April 20, 1963, the tasks, training, methodology, and requirements for the qualification of prospective candidates were outlined for the unit. They included "the belief in the victoriousness of socialism"; the complete knowledge of weapons, communications; the ability to engage in close combat, airborne operations;, and driving different types of vehicles. Knowledge as a radio operator, combat medicine, foreign languages, and training to be a combat diver were also required.

The training for the operators included:
- planning and penetrating "enemy territory" by land, air and sea,
- setting up safe sites and areas behind enemy lines,
- behavior in front of enemy security forces during interrogations,
- escape and evasion,
- mining, sabotage, demolition, attacks on individual vehicles and columns,
- recognizing and setting up ambushes, barriers and traps,
- means and options for eliminating enemy posts and individuals,
- raids of military headquarters facilities,
- capture and interrogation of prisoners.

Training was an option for operational employees of the various MfS departments, including the HVA. A military background was considered advantageous. Training was also open to suitable members of the MfS Guard Regiment "Feliks E. Dzierzynski."

The AGM/S was renamed Department XXII around 1988 as was given responsibility for counterterrorism operations. Ironically, this section also provided training to terror groups and individual terrorists who targeted West Germany including the Red Army Faction group.

SF Berlin Paratrooper, 1961 (credit: J. Wilde)   SF Berlin Training, 1987 (credit: Les Thaxton)

U.S. Army Special Forces Berlin

In the mid-1950s, Berlin was the epicenter of the Cold War conflict between the West and the East. The continued presence of Allied forces in the city was a "thorn in the side" of the communists and the goal of both the USSR and the GDR was to force the Allies to abandon the city so that it could be fully incorporated into East Germany. Simultaneously, the Allies deliberated on how best to maintain their presence, ensure unrestricted access to the city, and guarantee freedoms for West Berliners.

Militarily, Allied forces in Berlin were initially just regarded as a show garrison to "keep the flag flying" and to uphold the Four-Power status of the city as set out in the four-power agreements of 1945. In 1955, however, the US Commander of Berlin (USCOB) began to reassess that position and planned not only for a unified defense of the city with the British and French, but a possible break-out to the West. In the fall of 1955, the USCOB proposed that portions of the U.S. garrison in Berlin should prepare for such a contingency in conjunction with Special Forces operations in and around the city.

At a strategic conference in that same year, the three Allied Chiefs of Staff and the three Allied Commandants of Berlin agreed that demolition squads should be used to destroy strategic targets

Entrance Andrews Barracks, 1967 (credit: R. Sherman)

SF Berlin Hqs, Andrews Barracks, Building 904, 1976 (credit: D. Snow)

Entrance Andrews Barracks, now BundesArchiv, 2024 (credit: author)

outside the city to slow the Warsaw Pact should the Soviets choose to advance on the West.[12] U.S. Army planners recognized that if SF elements were stationed in Berlin before hostilities, they would be "behind the lines" as soon as hostilities began. Better still, they would have time to prepare for a possible Warsaw Pact D-Day in their operational area. Under the concept, the SF teams would destroy strategic targets outside the city to destabilize the enemy and retard his movements. Commander in Chief, US Army Europe agreed and, in November 1955, plans were made to assign six U.S. Army SF "A" teams to Berlin Command.[13]

The teams arrived in the summer of 1956 and for the next 35 years, until the fall of the Wall in 1989, they prepared for war. Their headquarters was located in Building 904 on Andrews Barracks in Lichterfelde from 1956 until 1984 (now home to an office of the *Bundesarchiv* or BA).[14] One of the

---

[12] The British and French occasionally deployed small special forces elements to Berlin but none were permanently assigned to the city.

[13] Headquarters, U.S. Army Europe, *The U.S. Army in Berlin, 1945-1961,* AG TS 2-102, (Heidelberg: USAREUR, 1963), 54-55 - Declassified 11 Dec 2000. While the deployment of Special Forces units fell under the responsibilities of USAREUR, command and control of operations was the responsibility of the Commander-in-Chief, US European Command (CINCEUR).

[14] Building 904 was demolished to make room for the archives of the East German Government.

SF Berlin Hqs Building 817, Roosevelt Barracks, Gardeschutzenweg (credit: author)

Practice Combat Diver Helo-cast at Andrews-Finckensteinallee Pool, 1960 (credit: J. Wilde)

Bundesnachrichtendienst entrance to Gardeschutzenweg (credit: author)

amenities that the unit enjoyed (besides an underground pistol range) was the 50-meter pool that was used for training and testing the unit's combat divers and their equipment.

The unit underwent a chameleon-like transformation in 1984 and reappeared at Haus 817 on Roosevelt Kaserne (now home to a sub-office of the *Bundesnachrichtendienst* or BND).

The small Allied occupation army in Berlin would be little more than an annoyance to the massive Group of Soviet Forces Germany, it could serve as delaying force to slow their advance. It was with this intent that the idea of placing a Special Forces Detachment in Berlin, 110 miles behind the Iron Curtain, was conceived. Although the unit was part of the occupation forces in Berlin, its mission was not defensive. It was a secret weapon ready to strike the heart of the Soviet Army at any moment.

In 1974, SF Berlin was given an additional mission as U.S. Army Europe's Counterterrorism force. The unit participated in the 1980 Iran hostage rescue mission and several other special operations before it was disbanded in 1990 after the Wall came down.[15]

— BA, Finckensteinallee 63, Lichterfelde, S-Bahnhof Lichterfelde-West (S1), S-Bahnhof Lichterfelde-Ost (S25/S26)

— BND-Außenstelle in Lichterfelde, Gardeschützenweg 71-101, S-Bahnhof Botanischer Garten (S1), Busstop Asternplatz (M48)

---

[15] Stejskal, James, Special Forces Berlin: Clandestine Cold War Operations of the US Army's Elite, 1956-1990, Oxford: Casemate, 2017.

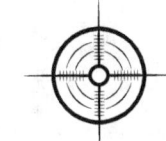

CHAPTER III
Blockade & Air Lift

"You peoples of the world, you peoples in America, in England, in France, in Italy! Look at this city and realize that you must not and cannot abandon this city and this people! There is only one possibility for all of us: to stand together until this battle is won, until this battle is finally sealed by victory over the enemies, by victory over the power of darkness."— Ernst Reuter in front of the Reichstag, 9. September 1948

By the end of 1947 Soviet obstructionism had brought the four-power governments' attempts to cooperatively administer Germany and Berlin to a standstill. Attempts to establish democratic institutions and self-government in the East were also impeded by the Soviet-controlled Socialist Unity Party or SED, the ruling communist party in East Germany. The breaking point came in March 1948 when the Soviet Military Governor, Marshal Sokolowsky, walked out of the Allied Control Council. This shattered the remnant of four-power government for all Germany.[16]

The Soviet presence in the Allied Kommandatura continued until 18 June 1948 when it ended with a Soviet walk-out. On 2 July, the Soviets formally notified the Western chiefs of staff that the Soviet Union had terminated participation in the Kommandatura.[17]

The Soviet's had already begun the Blockade of Berlin in an attempt to force the Western Allies out of the city.

---

[16] The Allied Control Council also referred to as the Four Powers, was the governing body of the Allied occupation zones in Germany (1945–1949/1991) and Austria (1945–1955) after WWII in Europe.
[17] The Allied Kommandatura was the governing body for the city of Berlin following Germany's defeat.

Tempelhof Airfield Today (credit: Allied Museum Berlin - Chodan)

From July 1945 through March 1948, the Soviets had persistently blocked Allied efforts to introduce economic reforms. At the Potsdam Conference, the Western Allies had not agreed to either the indefinite occupation of Germany or to its permanent division, but they were committed to promoting its economic recovery through the Marshall Plan.

The Allies decided to implement the needed reforms in the Western Zones of Occupation without the Soviets. On 16 June 1948 the new "Deutsche Mark" was introduced in West Germany and two days later into the Western Sectors of Berlin. That measure triggered the Soviet blockade. Before the blockade, Berlin was supplied largely by rail from the Western Zones. On 21 June the Soviets used the excuse of "technical difficulties" to cut rail communications. Access by road was also blocked. The Soviet Government wanted to starve Berliners and force the Western Allies to withdraw from Berlin.

What followed was an unprecedented use of air power by the Allies. When the first supply planes landed in Berlin on 26 June 1948, no one knew how long it would last or if it would work. But the Soviets were clearly violating international agreements and the U.S. Commandant of Berlin General Lucius Clay advised President Truman that the Berliners preferred hardship to communist rule.

The Berlin Airlift was on and the Allies along with the city's residents share the credit for its success. To supply a city of over two million people necessitated amazing organization on the ground. Military personnel supervised a German workforce of thousands. Army engineers constructed a new runway at Tempelhof in 49 days. On the site of a former German training area, they constructed a

C-47 "Skytrain" aircraft being unloaded during the height of the Blockade (credit: U.S. Airmobility Command)

A C-54 "Skymaster" aircraft, nicknamed the "Rosinen Bomber" or "Candy Bomber" at Tempelhof Open House, 1984. (credit: author)

new airfield, which became Tegel International Airport. Gatow Airfield, as well as the big lakes in the western part of the city all served as landing areas.

During this first "Cold War" battle for Berlin, most training and other activities were stopped as the complete manpower of the Allied garrisons in Berlin was employed in the airlift operation.

The Blockade lasted for some 324 days. It was finally ended with the Jessup-Malik agreement on 12 May 1949. Operation VITTLES (the airlift codename) continued for another two months while ground transportation was restored and stocks in the city returned to normal levels.

It was Berlin's first major post-war crisis and changed many Berliners' mind about the true nature of the Allied soldiers. Instead of seeing the Western Allies as occupation forces, they now saw them as saviors and protectors.

— Luftbrücke Memorial, U-Bahnhof Platz der Luftbrücke (U6), Bus (248, M43).

Platz der Luftbrücke memorial (credit: author)

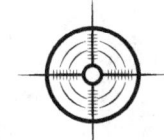

CHAPTER IV:
Aktion Rose or then came *Die Mauer* — The Berlin Wall

"A shadow has fallen upon the scenes lighted by the Allied victory. Nobody knows what Soviet Russia …intends to do in the immediate future, or what are the limits, if any, to their expansive tendencies. It is my duty to place before you certain facts about the present situation in Europe. From Stettin in the Baltic, to Trieste in the Adriatic, an Iron Curtain has descended across the continent. Behind that line lie all the capitals of the ancient states of Central and Eastern Europe – Warsaw, Berlin, Prague, Vienna, Budapest, Belgrade, Bucharest and Sofia. All these famous cities are subject to a very high and increasing measure of control from Moscow… This is certainly not the liberated Europe we fought to build up." — Winston Churchill, 5 March 1946 at Westminster College, Fulton, Missouri

"Nobody has the intention of building a wall" — Walter Ulbricht, East German SED Party 1st Secretary, June 1961

"Berliners wake to divided city." — BBC News headline, August 14, 1961

In 1952, the borders between the Soviet-supported German Democratic Republic (GDR/DDR) and the Allied-supported Federal Republic of Germany (FRG/BRD) were closed by a hard frontier barrier.

Nine years later, on August 13, 1961, the scene changed dramatically once more as, suddenly, the East German government closed access between East and West Berlin. It was a surprise to almost everyone, but certainly to the citizens of the city, who were cut off from their jobs, friends, and more importantly, their families. It was also a violation of the Potsdam Treaty. But would its construction lead to war? For a long while, no one was certain.

Day One - Construction Begins, 13 October 1961 (credit: NARA 13.10.1961 306-bn-114-h-38285)

Up until that day, it had been possible for Germans to travel relatively freely between the sectors of Berlin. People in the Soviet sector could work in the British, French, or American sector and many did. Some from the western sector worked in the East, but far fewer as the pay and conditions were inferior. The GDR's political system, ostensibly democratic but in reality anything but, as well as an all-pervasive police and security apparatus, including the massive Ministry for State Security (MfS), were factors that drove its citizens to distrust and fear their government and pushed them to escape. This, as well as West Germany's Basic Law that stated "any Germans" who could reach its territory had the right to a passport and social services on arrival, were all powerful incentives for East Germans to leave their homes and head for the economically stable West.

And they did. By the thousands, driving the GDR towards economic failure as many of the best and brightest fled. By 1961, an estimated 4 million East germans had escaped to the West. The leaders of the Soviet Union tried several times to force the Western Allies from Berlin, Josef Stalin with an total economic blockade in 1949, and again in 1958, when Nikita Khrushchev issued an ultimatum threatening to renounce the Potsdam Agreement that created a divided Berlin in the first place. Finally in 1961, Khrushchev demanded a peace treaty to reunite Germany under Communist terms, something the western allies refused to do.

The four occupying powers continued to haggle and negotiate, but the matter was finally settled on August 12, 1961, when Socialist Unity Party First Secretary, Walter Ulbricht, secretly ordered the closure of the border and a wall to be built.

Day One - NVA troops man a BTR-40 at Brandenburg Gate. (credit NARA 306-bn-114-h-38288)

NVA Grenztruppen armed with Soviet Ppsh-41 sub-machineguns on the Spree River, 1961 (credit: NARA 306-bn-95-4)

August 13, 1961

On the night of 13-14 August 1961, East German NVA soldiers, policemen, and militia men were alerted and moved in place to secure the crossing points between East and West in what the GDR's leadership called *Aktion Rose* or "Operation Rose."

Construction crews began to string barbed wire along the entire inner-city border, blocking all roads, tracks, and pathways into West Berlin. Soon the entire city was enclosed inside 97 miles of fence and wall, 27 of those split Berlin down the middle from North to South.

It was a day that would define an era.

An artist described the Wall as something a bunch of drunk stonemasons might have built and when first constructed it was a haphazard affair, but it was improved incrementally and made even more secure as the years went by. The outermost wall of the inner-city barrier, that is the part that faced West Berlin, was placed just inside GDR territory and was reinforced with additional obstacles to form a security zone in some places 100 meters wide. That meant that streets were closed and buildings sealed to prevent people from crossing the frontier.

The Wall successfully separated friends and family, 1961 (credit: NARA 306-bn-104-3)

A New Yorker article written by John Bainbridge one year after it was built described the Wall like this:

"It runs along the sector border…, which follows some of Berlin's old borough borders, is even more eccentric than most territorial boundaries, the wall runs a highly irregular course, going for a certain distance in one direction, veering off in another, curving slightly here, making a ninety-degree turn there, cutting through parks, squares, cemeteries, factory lots, and waterways, and continuing thus on its ragged way."[18]

Over the following days and months, the barrier would be tested by citizens and governments alike. For the western powers, the Wall illegally restricted their freedom of movement to East Berlin. For the people, it meant lost jobs and opportunities. By 1962, the Wall — called the "Anti-fascist Protection Barrier by the GDR — had become a permanent fixture and would remain so for 28 more years.

Initially, it was a collection of materials, barbed wire fences around the outskirts of West Berlin that prevented access from East Germany proper, and concrete block walls or blocked off buildings along the inner-city border. It was guarded by the *Grenztruppen* or Border Troops patrolling on foot or vehicles and in towers every hundred meters of so. Most importantly, they had orders to shoot anyone attempting to flee their homeland, which had just become a prison.

The GDR government issued the following directive to its frontier troops:

---

[18] John Bainbridge, "Die Mauer," *The New Yorker* magazine, October 19, 1962.

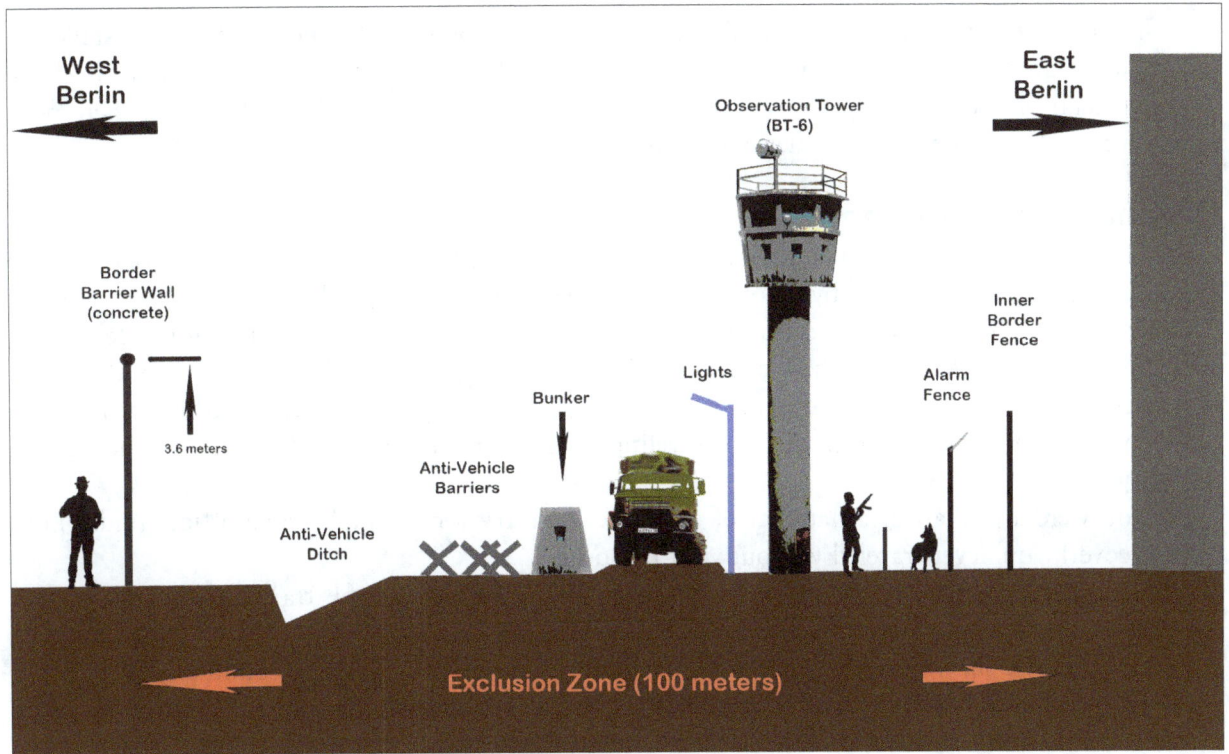

Berlin Wall Cross-section Diagram as it stood, circa 1985 (credit: author)

"Firearms must be used against traitors and border violators. Measures must be taken to ensure that criminals can be arrested within the 100-meter exclusion zone. Observation and firing ranges must be created within the exclusion zone."[19]

To make things even clearer, the City Commandant of East Berlin NVA General Helmuth Poppe reportedly ordered, **"No border violator may reach West Berlin alive."**

For the CIA, SIS, and DGSE, the Wall made spying in East Berlin much more difficult. For the MfS, KGB, and GRU it only complicated things a bit because, like mice, they found or made loopholes they could sneak through into the West. After all, the East Germans were in charge of it.

What The Wall Was

It was an evolving fortification. In 1961, building started just inside the actual trace of the East Berlin / East German sector with barbed wire laid on the ground. Then came more permanent structures like fences and concrete block walls. These barriers were improved and replaced as weaknesses were discovered — usually in the form of a successful escape. Ditches were added in some areas to frustrate anyone from trying to dig a tunnel. That said, there were a number of successful tunnels escapes. Sadly, there were more tunnels compromised and the would-be escapees either arrested or killed.

---

[19] *"Punkt 8, Befehl über die Gewährleistung der Sicherheit an der Westgrenze der DDR vom 20. September 1961"* - translated: Point 8, Order on Ensuring Security on the Western Border of the GDR of 20 September 1961

Unlike the frontier between the GDR and the BRD, anti-personnel mines were never installed in the exclusion area of the Berlin Wall. Besides the fences and concrete walls, barbed-wire, anti-vehicle ditches, metal obstacles (tetrahedrons), were the only physical barriers. Then, of course, there were towers manned with observers (soldiers with guns) and often dogs.

Getting Out & Getting In

If you were a U.S., U.K., or French diplomat or soldier, getting into West Berlin entailed one of three methods. First, you could travel by air on one of the three airlines permitted to fly in (Pan Am, British Air, Air France). If you wanted to travel by automobile, there was the Autobahn from Helmstedt, West Germany (Checkpoint Alpha) to the Dreilinden crossing (Checkpoint Bravo) in southwestern West Berlin. Last, you could hop on one of the three military duty trains that moved back and forth between West Berlin and West Germany. Traveling by train or car required Flag Orders issued by the respective military command.

If you were a civilian or a national of any other country (or an intelligence officer under non-official cover), you never traveled without your passport.

Getting into East Berlin from West Berlin meant using one of the transit points designated specifically for foreigners, West Germans, West Berliners, or diplomats and soldiers. The approved crossing points are shown on the map. Non-approved crossing points could be found anywhere along the Wall and could be used anytime by anyone with or without travel documents or approval, but there was an attendant risk of being shot by an East German Border Guard.

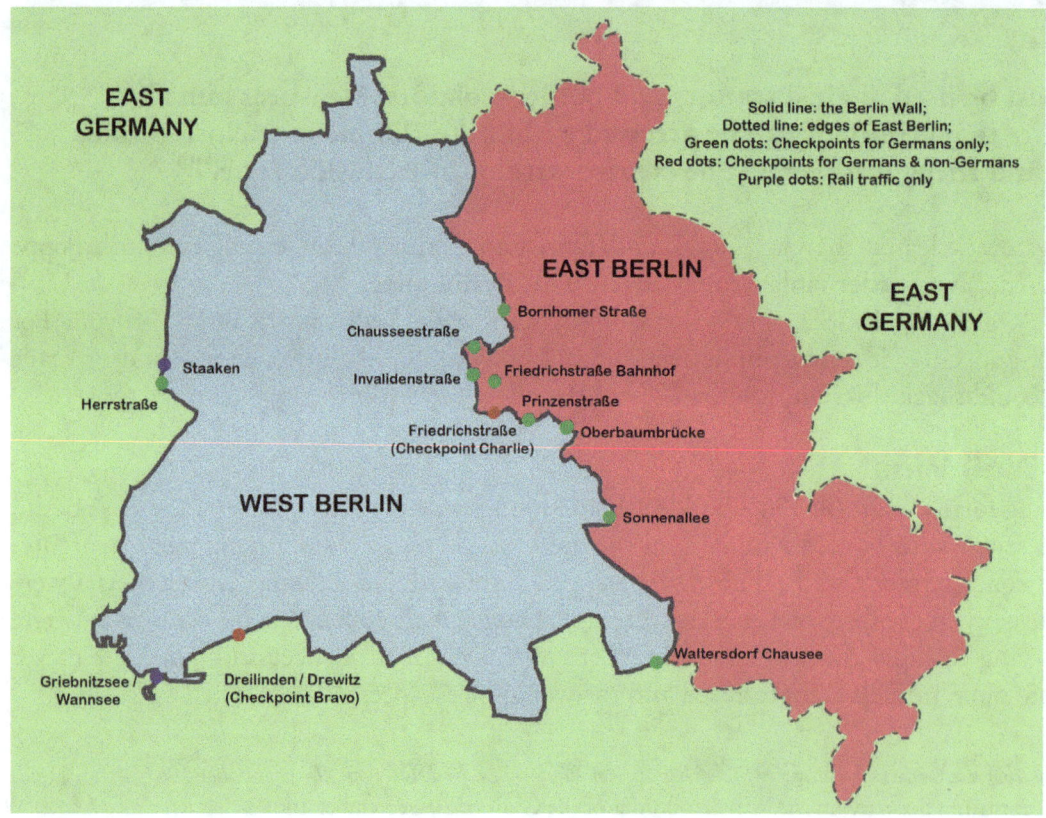

Official City Crossings Map (credit: author)

BT-11 Tower and Grenztruppen Motorcycle, 1985 (credit: author)

An early tower on the western border between West Berlin and East Germany, 1965 (credit: J.M. Kelly)

Watch Tower on Inner-city Border, 1977 (credit: author)

"Death Strip" in Frohnau (French Sector) between West Berlin and East Germany. (credit: author)

Grenztruppen truck visits a tower, 1987 (credit: author)

The varied transport available to the Border Troops (credit: author)

Border troops taking care of the guard dogs, 1985 (credit: author)

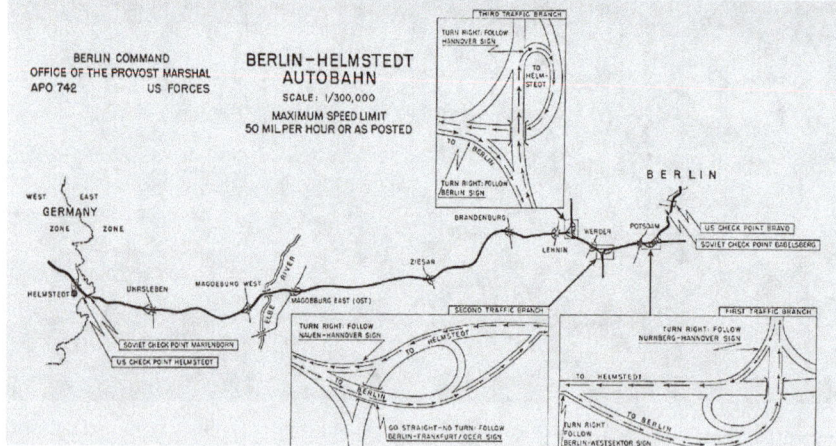

How to drive to Berlin from West Germany - Checkpoint Alpha to Check Bravo Autobahn Map (credit: U.S. Army)

Day One of Wall Construction at Checkpoint Charlie, 13 Aug 1961 (credit: NARA 306-bn-95-6)

Checkpoint Charlie

"Charlie" was the last in line of three official check points, the others being Check Point Alpha at the Helmstedt Autobahn border crossing between West Germany and East Germany, and Check Point Bravo at the Dreilinden Autobahn entry into West Berlin.

It was the most famous of all the crossing points. Located in the southern or American Sector of West Berlin, it was the location of several confrontations between the Soviets and the Americans in the early days of the Wall and became a symbol of the Cold War separation of East and West.

"In October 1961, Checkpoint Charlie (*Grenzübergangsstelle Friedrich / Zimmerstraße* to the East Germans) was the focal point of the deepening crisis over the Four-Power status of Berlin and catapulted it into world prominence. At issue was an East German attempt to deny free, uncontrolled entry into the Soviet Sector to civilian members of the forces in Berlin. They demanded that persons not actually in uniform identify themselves. Since status as members of the forces in Berlin derived from Allied laws agreed to by the Four Powers, and confirmed by long-standing precedents, the attempt to exclude civilian officials directly affected Allied rights. Then as now, "members of the forces," including military personnel, civilian employees and their dependents were prohibited from submitting to East German controls. The issues involved were complex and were not fully resolved until 1966. However, U.S. authorities in Berlin supported by General Lucius D. Clay were convinced that East German attempts to actually deny entry into East Berlin could not go unchallenged.[20] As a result, U. S. forces in the Checkpoint area were reinforced with tanks and armored personnel carriers

---

[20] The former U. S. Military Governor for Germany (1947-49), General Clay returned to Berlin in September 1961 as President Kennedy's personal representative with ambassadorial rank.

Confrontation: Soviet tanks Face Off against the Americans at Check Point Charlie, 26 October 1961 (credit: H.D. Halterman)

(APC); one of the APCs and two tanks were positioned north of the Checkpoint building right at the S/S demarcation line."

"Beginning on 26 October, U.S. forces registered vehicles denied entry into East Berlin because non-uniformed personnel refused to identify themselves, were given an armed escort of jeep-mounted Military Police and sent back through the crossing point. Neither Soviet authorities nor East German police attempted to stop the escorted vehicles. By 1700 hours the next day, however, Soviet troops and armor had moved into position on their side of the S/S line. During the ensuing 24 hours, foreign and diplomatic travelers continued to move unmolested through the checkpoint. Until approximately 1100 hours on 28 October, Soviet and U. S. troops and tanks faced each other across the Friedrichstrasse boundary. At that time, both Soviet and U. S. forces withdrew into nearby staging areas on their respective sides. Inherent in the civilian-identification issue was the Four-Power status of Greater Berlin. The Western Allies insisted, in the face of Soviet disclaimers, that the Soviet Union remain responsible for its Sector. The firm U. S. position on the issue led to a Soviet demonstration, documented world-wide by the news media, of its ultimate responsibility for events in East Berlin. While the confrontation was in progress, General Clay called a news conference and pointedly announced the significance of the events then taking place: "The fiction that it was the East Germans who were responsible for trying to prevent Allied access to East Berlin is now destroyed. The fact that Soviet tanks appeared on the scene proves that the harrassments. . . taking place at Friedrichstrasse were not those of the self-styled East German government but ordered by its Soviet masters."[21]

The site has been represented in many movies and books, most notably *The Spy Who Came in from the Cold* and James Bond in the film *Octopussy*.[22] There is a museum located nearby that contains a full history of the Wall and many of the escape attempts.

— Checkpoint Charlie, Friedrichstraße and Kochstraße, U-Bahnhof Kochstraße (U6), Bus stop U-Bahn Kochstraße/Checkpoint Charlie (M29, N6)

---

[21] *USCOB/USAB Pam 870-1: Checkpoint Charlie.*

[22] The Stasi was very interested in James Bond as they photographed the *Octopussy* film set at CP Charlie extensively from one of their guard towers.

President J.F. Kennedy visits Berlin. USCOB
General Watson rides with to meet West Berlin
Mayor Willi Brandt. (credit: H.D. Halterman)

Confrontation from the US Point of View.
(credit: NARA 306-bn-100-3)

Checkpoint Charlie 1967
(credit: Roger Sherman)

Checkpoint Charlie 1988
(credit: Robert Schreiber)

Friedrichstraße Bahnhof across River Spree from Ganymed Grill, 2024. (credit: author)

Stasi "Grenzschleuse" Border Crossing at Friedrichstraße (credit: BStU, MfS, ZAIG, Fo, Nr. 2543, Bild 9)

Slipping Spies Through the Wall — Friedrichstraße Bahnhof & Tränenpalast

Along with the few official crossing points from East to West, the Friedrichstraße Bahnhof was home to the *Tränenpalast* or "Palace of Tears," so named because it was the point of separation for many families whose members were traveling to the West and might not be seen again for a long time.

After the construction of the Berlin Wall in 1961, members of the MfS / Stasi also had to negotiate these borders, but they often wanted to do so without exposing their HVA officers or agents. Along the East German (GDR) and West German (FRG) border a wide restricted area made up of guards, controls, signal fences, border towers, and minefields had to be crossed. In order to be able to cross the mined border strip safely, the MfS kept precise maps.

It was said they had fewer problems passing through border controls in the West Germany than they did in the East. Markus Wolf, the head of Stasi's foreign intelligence department, the HVA, set up a working group to find the best way to get his officers and agents back and forth across the Wall with the minimum of problems. Soon the *MfS* had established official smuggling points along the East and West German border as well as into West Berlin. Each crossing points was given its own code name.

Until the end of 1989, the State Security Service used the border smuggling points to send agents on special missions into the Federal Republic of Germany. Remnants of the former border strip and the Iron Curtain can still be clearly seen in the landscape today. The secret gates to the West, however, disappeared soon after reunification.

— Friedrichstraße Bahnhof (S1 S2, S3, S5, S7, S9, S25, RE21, RE29), Tram (M1, 12)

Compromised Escape Tunnel at Bernauerstraße & Eberswalderstraße, 1964. (credit: Roger Sherman)

Reconstruction of Tunnel 29 Entrance at Brunnenstrasse 137-141. (credit: ©Berliner Unterwelten e.V. / Holger Happel)

Going Under: Tunnels — Bernauer Straße

From the early days of the Berlin Wall, there were repeated attempts to gain freedom by crossing the deadly frontier through the urban sewer system or self-dug tunnels. The first tunnel began in October 1961, the last attempt — a failure — was in 1982. In total, more than 70 tunnels were started; only 19 were successful. That said, 300 East Germans managed to make it to West Berlin and freedom.

There were spectacular successes, betrayals and bitter failures. Soon, a veritable "cat and mouse game" developed between the tunnel builders and the GDR State Security, with increasingly difficult conditions for the escape helpers and refugees. From 1961 to 1989 over 140 persons died attempting to escape.

Underground Berlin is a fascinating place with "ghost" U-Bahn stations and nearly impenetrable security against so-called *Verräter* und *Grenzverletzer* (traitors and border violators), which went so far as to seal off of the sewage system against underground escape attempts.

Bernauer Straße is a focal point for these escapes as, over a lateral distance of just 350 meters along the Wall, seven tunnel escape attempts — several very successful — were made. The exceptionally low ground water level made the creation of deeper escape tunnels possible.

One of the best places to start is with a visit to the underground tunnels. It begins with a visit to the exhibition rooms in an underground civil defense facility in Blochplatz. After traveling by "subway shuttle" to Bernauer Strasse, the guided adventure continues in the cellars of the former Oswald-Berliner Brewery, a hotspot during the building of the Wall and a focal point in escape tunnel construction. Betrayed and failed tunnel projects, as well as the two most successful and spectacular projects from the time of the Berlin Wall — Tunnel 29 and Tunnel 57 — are discussed by the tour guides and one surviving tunnel can be visited. Additionally, the German 2001 documentary of the construction of a tunnel, *The Tunnel,* by Roland Suso Richter is well worth your time.

— Berliner Unterwelten e.V., (Contact: https://www.berliner-unterwelten.de/en/index.html)

— Berlin Wall Memorial, (See: https://www.stiftung-berliner-mauer.de/en/berlin-wall-memorial)

Berliner underground - sewer system, 1974. (credit: MG Sidney Shachnow)

Glienecke Bridge, 1980.
(credit: Ladislav Szilagi)

Glienecke Bridge, 2024.
(credit: author)

Glienicker Brücke — the Bridge of Spies

Glienicke Bridge was built in 1907 to replace the wooden and brick bridge that previously joined Berlin to the suburb of Potsdam. Heavily damaged by a bomb at the end of WWII, it was repaired and used primarily by the U.S., U.K., and French as a link between their Berlin headquarters sections and their respective military liaison missions in Potsdam.

Initially open for traffic between West Berlin and Potsdam, the bridge was closed in 1952 to citizens of West Berlin and the FRG. After the Berlin Wall was put in place on 13 August 1961, citizens of the GDR could not use it. Despite that, for propagandistic reasons the East Germans named it the "Bridge of Unity."

A long dispute on the cost of repair and renovation ensued between West Berlin and the GDR. The half on the West Berlin side was repaired in 1980 and, after the Senate declared that it would pay for the repairs needed on the East German / Potsdam side, the other half was renovated in 1985. In return, the GDR agreed to change the name back to "Glienicke Bridge."

In 1988 three citizens of Potsdam spectacularly broke through the border in a lorry, but several other attempts ended in failure.

— Glienicker Bridge, Königstraße / Berliner Straße 77–81, S-Bahn (S7) to Potsdam Hauptbahnhof via Tram (93) or Bus (N16) to Schloss Glienicke.

Memorial marker to the division of Berlin (credit: author)

Bridge of Spies at Night, 2024 (credit: Opti)

CHAPTER V
Tradecraft - Getting things done...

Whatever it's called, spying, espionage, or human intelligence, the craft requires commitment and devotion. An intelligence officer must be devoted to doing the things required of him or her to accomplish the mission. One American intelligence officer stated that he "devoted [his] life to protecting our country against totalitarian, evil, oppressive, atheistic communism, and we thought we were on the right side of that."[23]

Many intelligence officers consider Thomas Aquinas' "Just War Theory" to be a guiding moral code. That theory states essentially that it is morally acceptable to kill in legitimate defense of your country. If killing is acceptable then so are lying, cheating, manipulation, and deceiving to accomplish your mission.

I'm sure Russian and Chinese officers have their own version of what motivates them to do the work. Work that often requires them to have no qualms or reservations about doing what they need to do for their country.

The tools of espionage are what the intelligence community calls "Tradecraft" — the tactics, techniques, and procedures used in its operations. They are the tricks of the trade so to speak. But in most cases they aren't tricks. They are tried and tested methods to get a job done. Many of the methods used are variations of techniques devised years ago by practitioners of the world's "second oldest profession." Others, especially technical means, have only come into use recently.

Users of any of these techniques must always be cautious and continually ask themselves if they are being overly reliant on a certain method or if a certain tactic has been used too often. If they don't, they're liable to find out that reliance on just one technique can be dangerous and one slip-up can lead to a cascade of failures that can destroy an entire network. The danger lies with an organization that

---

[23] James Mohler, "Spycraft and Soulcraft on the Front Lines of History: A Conversation with Former CIA Chief of Counterintelligence James Olson," retrieved from https://albertmohler.com/2021/04/28/james-olson/

comes up with "the solution to a problem" and thinks itself equipped with a passkey to keep it totally safe from discovery. The CO (case officer), the spy, the leadership must never become complacent.

Current technology has been seen as the solution to clandestine commo but we have seen massive network compromises because of over-reliance on tech. The Arab Spring is a good example, where "revolutionaries" relied on internet and cellular telephone-based social media (SM) to communicate quickly with large groups of people. Unfortunately, the repressive governments of Libya, Iran, and Syria capitalized on the incautious use of SM to trace members and suppress them. People often believe sending encrypted messages will protect them, but the monitors who analyze that traffic will often decide that anyone who sends a message they can't read must have something to hide and will act accordingly. About the only technical communications method that is difficult for the opposition to counter or trace are the so-called "numbers stations" that send encrypted short-wave radio messages from outside the country to agents inside. Knowing who is receiving those messages and what they say is nearly impossible.

CCTV and biometric technologies have thrown additional challenges at clandestine operators, challenges that mostly didn't exist in the Cold War. The assumption is that the intelligence officer and the agent must assume they are being listened to or surveilled (watched) at all times.

Finally, any communications technique used must fit the life-style of the asset and the case officer. It should not require them to do anything that is not consistent with their daily patterns or their cover — if they have one. If they have to leave their comfort zone, their "bubble" of safety, they must be very careful, even paranoid. Remember, just because you are paranoid, doesn't mean "they" are not watching! Any tool has advantages and disadvantages, risks and gains; it is up to the craftsman – the officer and the agent – to know which to use and when.

Working in a so-called "denied area" makes being a spy difficult if not deadly. A denied area simply put, is an extremely hostile environment where the opposition controls everything and has an efficient security service with very good surveillance capabilities. The Soviet Union (now Russia), China, Cuba, Iran, North Korea all fall into that category. East Germany (and East Berlin) with its all pervasive internal security apparatus was at the extreme end of the designation "denied area." Even the relatively free cities of London and Prague, among others, are covered by "pervasive' surveillance systems.

Cover

Case Officers, intelligence officers, and agents in general, need a reason to be wherever they are located, as well as one to move about the area. The first is called a Cover for Status. Agents also known as Spies, usually don't have a Cover of Status. As Yogi Berra might have put it, "They are what they are." Whether a scientist working at a laboratory or a military officer assigned to a headquarters, they live a natural cover. It's what they normally do, but now they have a second life they must hide from everyone else.

Official Cover

An officer of an intelligence agency cannot arrive in a denied area (or even an allied country) and announce that he works for the CIA, SIS, KGB, or the Chinese MSS. He must have another job title to keep his intelligence activities under wraps. He or she might be covered as a government official at an embassy with diplomatic privileges and immunity. That is Official Cover and it is the safest way for an intelligence officer to work in a foreign country because they generally will not be imprisoned if caught — just thrown out of country as *persona non grata* — in accordance with international law. Embarrassing yes, but still alive.

Non-official Cover

An agent or officer working for a commercial company, as a journalist, a scientist, or even a tourist is under Non-official Cover (NOC).[24] The Soviets (and now the Russians) called these agents "Illegals."[25] Prior to WWII, Soviet master-spy, Leon Trepper, created a NOC-organization called "The Foreign Excellent Raincoat Company" in Brussels, and KGB spy Emil Robert Goldfus (true name: William August Fisher) operated undercover for the KGB in the United States where he had arrived in 1948. Fisher was an important conduit for information on the atomic bomb secrets stolen from U.S. Manhattan Project. He was discovered through the defection of another illegal and arrested in 1957. When he was arrested, Fisher adopted the name Rudolf Ivanovich Abel, a dead Russian colonel and former friend, knowing that his KGB masters in Moscow would realize he had been captured when the name appeared in the news. Fisher was sentenced to 30 years in prison but served only four.In 1962, he was released and exchanged for American U-2 surveillance plane pilot, Francis Gary Powers, who had been shot down over the Soviet Union. The exchange took place across the Glienicke Bridge on February 10, 1962.[26] At the same moment, another American, Frederic Pryor, an economist arrested in East Berlin on trumped up charges of espionage in 1959, was released at Checkpoint Charlie. Some have described NOC agents as having the loneliest job in the world.

Cover for Action

Once the officer or agent has his cover for status, his "raison d'etre" to be in country then he must have reasons for the work he needs to do there, whether meeting with certain types of people or for perhaps traveling near a suspect facility at a certain time. That reason is called "Cover for Action." It might be meeting with officials or businessmen, shopping for antiques, taking photos of old churches, getting a haircut, or visiting a certain café, all are reasons for being at a location. A surveillance detection route might incorporate many of these "cover stops" strung together to make a long run to bore the people who are probably following you.

Moscow Rules

Common sense and a large amount of paranoia are required for operating in a denied area. The following are the Agency's "Moscow Rules" — the minimum requirements for keeping your backside

---

[24] The CIA and other U.S. intelligence agencies are mostly prohibited from using journalist or humanitarian worker as a cover.

[25] Russia probably still has illegals in the USA. As recently as 2010, 10 Russians illegals were arrested in the FBI's "Operation Ghost Stories."

[26] The incident was depicted in the 2015 film *Bridge of Spies*.

out of jail while working against the Russians. They were and are still applicable all over the world when working in denied areas (with comments).

1. Assume nothing. (They are trying to get you to make a mistake.)
2. Never go against your gut. (If it feels wrong, you're right.)
3. Everyone is potentially under opposition control. (Everyone!)
4. Never look back; you're never alone. (Don't tie shoes or look at reflections.)
5. Go with the flow, blend in. (Why is a man in the women's lingerie department?)
6. Vary your pattern and stay within your cover. (Do nothing new on an op. See next.)
7. Lull them into a sense of complacency. (Bore them to tears.)
8. Do not harass the opposition. (Makes them mad and they'll make you regret it.)
9. Pick the time and place for action. (Don't rush. Mind the gap. See below.)
10. Keep your options open. (Have an alternate plan or three.)

Moscow Rules are very different from London Rules, which are simple and to the point: "Cover your arse."[27]

Surveillance

If Surveillance is an art, Counter-surveillance is being an art critic.

A difficult skill to master, surveillance is observing and following a suspected person's daily routine and activities. Whether in criminal, marital, or espionage cases, surveillance is required to determine if a surveilled person might be involved in illegal or immoral activities. Sometimes it might be nothing more than a suspicion or the subject may be a known intelligence officer, spy, or criminal. The surveillants may be trying to catch them in the act of something or they may want to find out with whom they are working.

One of the first skills to be learned as an intelligence officer, and just one of many that must be taught to their own agents / spies, is surveillance and counter-surveillance. Surveillance must be learned not only as a skill to execute, but more importantly, as a tactic to be recognized and understood. Only then can opposition surveillance be beaten.

It's not a skill you can learn by reading a book. It requires some instruction (classroom or video) and then hours of on the street practice. A solo operator can do surveillance, but not for long before they get tired, lose their quarry, or get burned. Teams are much better because they can change up their routine, swap out members that get too close, and provide better coverage. Again it takes practice and excellent communications, whether by radio or hand signals. And more than anything, those doing the surveillance have to blend in and be the proverbial grey people.

Surveillance can be mobile — on foot, in a car, or maybe a drone. Or it can be a static post like a newspaper stand, apartment window, vendor, or food truck to monitor a specific person's place of work or home. One person may surveil a target but in intelligence operations, a basic surveillance team might be made up of four surveillants who would be called A, B, C, and D. Their objective is to follow the suspect / subject from directly behind as well as paralleling his/her movement. If the target is of high-value, a team might run as many as 30 surveillants and five to ten vehicles in support, based on how discreet the hostile service wishes to be. Obviously, a larger number equates to a greater possibility of discovery. But sometimes that's not the point. A close, obtrusive surveillance team might intend to

---

[27] With apologies to Mick Herron and Jackson Lamb.

rattle the suspect and either force them into doing something stupid or prevent them from conducting any operations altogether. As they say in the movies, "It depends."

Surveillance doesn't even need people and these days many cities are completely covered with technical means of surveillance. CCTVs to watch the public and even cellular telephones can be tracked inside buildings. Drones are also being used more frequently. Today, an intelligence officer or spy is as vulnerable to commercial surveillance as they are from hostile government overwatch. And remember, they might be in front of you or even overhead.

A counter-terrorist operation took place in Berlin that used motorcycles parked on the street with still and video cameras oriented on the entrances of public transit facilities known to have been used by suspects. The cameras captured hundreds of people's images which were compared with those from other locations. Showing up in both or all the sets of photographs was an indicator of illegal activity and facilitated identifying and ultimately arresting a number of terrorists. Sorting through the images took a lot of manpower and was an example of how much analysis is required to conduct an effective surveillance operation.

Stasi Surveillance of Suspects in a Car Park (credit: BStU HA VII, Fo444, Bild31)

Stasi Surveillance of old lady at Mail Box "Oma am Briefkasten" (credit: BStU HAXX 177)

U.S. surveillance - Rathaus Spandau U-Bahnhof U.S. surveillance, 1977 (credit: author)

Rathaus Spandau U-Bahnhof, 2024 (credit: Jonny Whitman)

Parked Moto - possible surveillance platform. (credit: author)

He looks innocuous., but is he? Surveillant on train platform. (credit: author)

USCOB 380-2 Security
Poster (credit: U.S. Army)

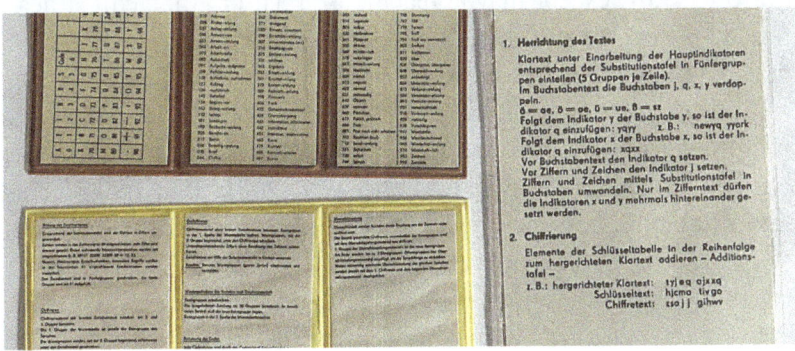

MfS *Stasi* Miniature Code Set
(credit: author)

Secret Talk — Clandestine Communications

Stationed in Berlin in the 1970s, we were trained in "non-technical communications" and other forms of intelligence tradecraft for what we called "urban operations."[28] NTC meant simply not using radios and in almost all cases no telephones to talk with each other clandestinely. Nearly all the public and private telephones in East Germany, East Berlin and many in the West were monitored. Telephones were dangerous. NTC is how to stay in contact with your assets, your team, or the command element, without compromising yourself or them. Operational security is paramount in a clandestine organization because if one member is identified, all members can be identified if good tradecraft is ignored. The opposition can identify a singleton (or solo) spy by watching and tracking (aka surveilling) the known intelligence officers who might handle them. Therefore, "cutouts" are usually necessary to eliminate that connection. A cut-out can be another trusted person or a dead-drop, anything that puts distance between one party and another.

An old spy once told me that he identified an opposition spy by following his Soviet handler day in and day out. It was when he determined the Russian was passing messages back and forth in fresh fish sold at a local market did he find the spy he was looking for.

---

[28] As opposed to "fieldcraft," which are those soldier skills that are necessary when wearing camouflage and carrying a rifle in the woods

Passing the Buck & Minding the Gap

Spies must be able to master the art of passing a message without the "pass" being seen by the opposition surveillance teams. One of the techniques taught was called the "brush pass." Essentially, it was a quick exchange to pass messages or materials from one person to another without being noticed or the two individuals being linked and compromised by the opposition. It was a carefully choreographed move that required planning and practice to get it right. You've probably seen it in a movie.

The guys who taught us were old hands, experienced officers who'd spent time on the streets in some of the more "interesting" cities around the world. Moscow, Bucharest, Vientiane were just a few of the fun spots mentioned as they related how they'd done exchanges under pressure.

Before we could do an exchange ourselves, we watched our mentors do it on the streets. Given photographs of the two participants we would be told to be at a vantage point and wait. Invariably, even knowing both players we would miss the pass. There was always a bit of magic in what they did, a sleight of hand not present in any other bit of tradecraft, except maybe placing a signal or emplacing a dead drop under pressure. One factor that made the action even harder to spot was called "using the gap."

The "gap" was another innovation developed not by the KGB or any other enemy intelligence organization but by a CIA officer who developed the technique on the streets of Prague in the late 1950s when the CIA was itself learning how to operate in the all-pervasive surveillance states of the Warsaw Pact. One of the key players in this process was Havilland Smith. One of his first assignments was Prague where he was part of a small staff that became even smaller when his co-worker was sent home after a nervous breakdown.

Smith became responsible for handling all the agents in country and spent a lot of time on the streets. Mostly he supported the agents already recruited. Information came by letter or was retrieved from dead-letter drops - secret "mail" left in hidden spots around the city. As he walked the streets of Prague, usually accompanied by a bunch of Czech intelligence officers who were watching his every move, he thought about the best ways to escape surveillance. His theories would later influence how tradecraft was used by the CIA.

But it was when he was posted to Berlin in 1960, that he really began to come up with creative ideas, especially after the Wall went up in 1961. He stated that:"It was a terrible time. It was just obvious how bankrupt the Soviet system was."

The Wall complicated his tasks and made it more difficult to operate, but it was in this environment that many new techniques of intelligence tradecraft were devised. To keep contact with his agents, Smith used dead drops and sent messages that were posted through accommodation addresses — a place in a denied area like East Berlin where a letter could be sent and then passed to an agent by a trusted cut-out.

Smith came back to the United States in 1963 and taught a course on how to work with contacts behind the Iron Curtain; and how to solve the biggest problem they then faced: "how to exchange information when being tailed."

Experience and failure had taught the agency how difficult it was to know "whether or not you're under surveillance." The answer was simple: you can't know; you must assume you're always under surveillance. So that begged the next question: How can an officer operate while under surveillance?

Smith came up with a method known as "exploiting the gap" to pull off his brush pass. He had noticed during his walks in Prague that he was often followed by at least four secret police agents, two directly behind him and two across the street. He found that when he turned a corner, the agents behind him would lose sight of him for a moment before they caught up and if he turned quickly around another corner, the gap would grow even larger. It was in this "gap" that he could meet his contact and pass a message or even load a dead-drop. He also found that his contact needed a way out, somewhere to disappear like into an alley or a shop, so the followers would not encounter him and suspect something had happened. With good planning and practice it would work.

Before any new method is used operationally, it must be approved. And so, Smith had to demonstrate his brainchild under the watchful gaze of two very senior CIA officers in the reception area of a large hotel. Watching the officer walk in front of them, one of the men asked when the show would begin. He was told that it had just happened and he had missed it. The brush pass method was approved and remains useful in denied areas around the world.[29]

Sending Signals

"Anne moved to a window and glanced toward West Berlin... Her building was there in the middle of the curving street. She took in the short distance of the divide, but then her eyes settled on the colored glass vases that sat on Petra's window sill. Five vases, five colors. She remembered Stefan's sketches.

'If I wanted to see him, I placed them in one order. If I had an urgent message, I placed them in a different order. We had a code. That's how we communicated'"
— Paul Vidich, *The Matchmaker*

Secret signals are used for a myriad of purposes, a signal might ask for a meeting or say a dead-drop has been loaded and needs servicing. These are called Activation Signals. And almost anything can be used as a signal, flower pots and curtains in windows, a chalk mark on a post box, a piece of tape on a light pole, a telephone call to a "wrong" number, or an advertisement in the newspaper. One of the key elements to be considered is timing. In today's world of texts and messaging, a message or signal can be sent instantly and reacted to just as quickly. Those messages can also be traced. But a physical message must be read and requires the recipient to see the message, so some kind of schedule is often helpful. The instructions for the signal might be to look for a particular mark at a certain site every day after 0900 (9 am). Easy enough, but that would require someone (the recipient) to pass by that spot every day. All kinds of factors must be thought of: timing, access (the site must open), availability of whatever mark or item is being used to make the signal.

Wherever you travel in Berlin, you will see thousands of suitable signal sites. Often these locations are marked with stickers and graffiti that mean little. But occasionally, there is a secret message among them that is meant to be read by a agent or a case officer.

---

[29] Benjamin Weiser in *A Secret Life:A Secret Life: The Polish Officer, His Covert Mission, and the Price He Paid to Save His Country.*

Signal Site - which mark is the Load Signal? (credit: author)

Marking a signal site. Traffic light provides cyclist with cover for action. (credit: author)

An ordinary stick turned into
Concealment Device - Before & After
(credit: author)

Flower pot - a possible
Dead Letter Drop
(credit: author)

Cache Can (aluminum) - When you
really need to store stuff underground
(credit: author)

Posting the Mail

"On the bench, next to the basket, he saw the yellow chalk mark he was looking for, running over two slats, bright as a canary, telling him that the handover had taken place successfully."— John Le Carré, *Smileys' People*

Dead-Letter Drops (DLD) or simply Dead Drops (DD) are a kind of secret post office, a place known only to the Case Officer handler and the agent that is used to leave a message or even a small package. A DLD can be used to pass information in either direction, that is, from the CO (higher) to the agent (lower) and vice versa. The amount of information an agent can put in a DLD is unlimited. A waterproof container could also be used. One spy (FBI Agent Robert Hansenn) used a trash bag that he stuffed under a pedestrian bridge in a park.[30]

To conduct a Dead Drop, the agent and the handler must both know what the package will look like, where it is to be located and the signals. A signal is used by the sender when the DLD is "loaded." When the recipient "unloads" it, he puts up a different signal. Under extreme circumstances, "Proceeding to load site" and a corresponding "Proceeding to unload" signals may be used. Then, if either the "load" or "unload" signals do not appear, the agent or the handler will know the operation has been compromised.

Another version of a Dead Drop is the Cache, usually a long-term secret storage site hidden in a building or buried underground. These are often used by underground resistance forces or stay-behind units in preparation for war. Berlin had and may still have (?) cache sites buried beneath its seemingly peaceful terrain.

---

[30] Another spy, a Russian, betrayed Hansenn who was arrested and died in prison.

The Personal Meet (PM)

Occasionally spies need to talk with their handler / case officer. Passing messages by radio, or through encrypted notes left in dead drops might take care of the intelligence needs and small details, but once in a while — whether to give specific details of an operation, motivate an agent, or assess his or her state of mind — direct conversation between handler and agent is necessary and a PM is the best way to accomplish the objective, but also dangerous as the meeting might be observed or reported.

Recognition and Safety Signals

Sometimes static signals are used even before the meeting to show an officer or agent that his partner is en route to the meeting and it is safe (at least from his point of view). This signal (maybe a chalk mark on a post) would be placed along the route before the meeting site to tell the other participant only that it's still scheduled to happen. In the case of a personal meet, an umbrella or a newspaper held in one hand or the other can be an agreed safety or recognition signal. The meeting can still be called off — "aborted" — at any moment with the absence of the safety signal by one or both of the participants at the actual meet site.

Personal Meet Site (PM) KaDeWe Bar
(credit: author)

Recognition Signal - One man with "Two Beers"
(credit: author)

Car Pick Ups (CPU)

A variant of the Personal Meet. Often used to avoid a static PM, the CPU requires good planning, timing, and signals. The pick-up location must be invisible (as much as possible) to surveillants who might be following either the handler or the agent, as must the drop off site. Most importantly are the signals which identify the pick-up vehicle and indicate danger. Getting in the wrong vehicle is not conducive to secure operations, although it makes for interesting war stories.

And Alway Paperwork...

As with all secret activity, good planning is required and whoever said that being a spy or even an intelligence officer was glamorous and full of excitement has never planned an operation. One saying that applies to intelligence work is this:

"It is hours and hours of boredom, punctuated by moments of sheer terror."

As with any bureaucracy, paperwork and records are required for the organization to function (whether properly or improperly depends on the observer). Not only for good security and continuity, keeping records of operational acts (meetings, dead-drops, signal sites, and such) reports are crucial. That way if something goes wrong, headquarters can "walk back the dog" in order to determine where a mistake might have been made. A typical circa mid-1970s report — in this instance, format for a surveillance detection route — is shown below.

CASING REPORT FORMAT

SURVEILLANCE DETECTION ROUTE

NOTE: INCLUDE ONLY NECESSARY, PERTINENT DATA. SPECIFY ONLY ASPECTS WHICH REQUIRE PARTICULAR ATTENTION OR THAT ARE PARTICULARLY RECOMMENDED.

LOCATION: CITY / BEZIRK(S) / SUBDIVISION

Example: BERLIN / ZEHLENDORF / DAHLEM

CODENAME: "EXAMPLE"

REPORT #: Only if you use a numbering system.

DATE PREPARED: Quick reference for currency of data

1. GENERAL LOCATION: Give map reference, page numbers, and edition, i.e. (Berlin Stadtatlas, pp. 45, 46, 56, Auflage 13.) encompassing the route.

2. SPECIFIC ROUTE: Describe concisely, but completely enough to insure that the route can be followed. Maximize the use of clearly, easily identifiable landmarks that are permanent. Route should require a minimum of two hours, including cover stops.

    a. Start Point

    b. Exact Route (maximize channeling and flow)

    c. End Point

3. COVER STOPS: Pinpoint location and any other pertinent details so that cover stops can be easily found. Specify if particular locales / areas within the cover stop (department of a large store, etc.) should be visited and for how long, if time is a consideration, Specify days/hours of operation at each cover stop. Specify which entrances/exits are to be used.

4. COUNTER-SURVEILLANCE POINTS: Specify at least four location(s) along tho route, to include all pertinent details so that the points can be easily found. Insure that the specific route (para 2) is designed to facilitate timely movement of counter-surveillants from one point to the next. If more than one counter-surveillant is used, designate which location will be used to exchange a safety signal between them. The final counter-surveillance point will be used to exchange the safety signal to the person walking / driving the route.

5. SAFETY SIGNALS: (Remember, absence of a safety signal means danger.)

    a. Counter-surveillant to the person walking / driving the route

    b. Counter-surveillant to counter-surveillant

6. COVER FOR ACTION: Describe in as much detail as required, Lb include cover stops or pauses. Cite any characteristics of the neighborhood(s) or cover stop locations that would influence cover (dress, props, etc). Describe cover for each participant, including counter-surveillants.

7. SECURITY CONSIDERATIONS: Describe all significant aspects along the entire routes to include traffic patterns (foot, vehicular), security forces, and watchful citizens. note any "hot spots" along/near the route.

8. OTHER CONSIDERATIONS

    a. Use factors:

        1) Days, hours, circumstances most suitable (opening/closing times)

        2) Days, hours, circumstances not suitable (any segment of the route)

    b. Influence of climate / season

    c. Anything significant, but not covered elsewhere in the report.

9. CASING HISTORY: Provide the name of person doing the casing and the date / time of the casing. Show how the casing was performed (foot, vehicle) and note any unusual circumstances that would afflict evaluation of the report.

MfS *Stasi* Surveillance - they even watched themselves (credit: BStU)

CHAPTER VI
Spies and Traitors

Intelligence tradecraft must be learned and practiced in order to be competent on the streets, but there is one other aspect of human intelligence operations that is equally, if not more important to understand. That is the art of agent recruitment and handling and it is worth a complete book in of itself.

One bit of terminology deserves discussion, What is a Spy?

A spy is "a person who secretly collects and reports information about the activities of another country or organization."[31] In most government intelligence organizations, a "spy" is an insider — a man or woman who provides secret information about his country or organization to another. That country might be the "enemy" or not. Sometimes "friendly" countries have secrets they don't wish to share but others wish to know about. The spy is usually a citizen of the country he's betraying.

The people who recruit and handle those spies — also called spooks, agents, assets, joes — are called intelligence or case officers and they normally are from another country. It's all semantics. For our purposes, they all deserve the name spy because they are all involved in illegal activities. The only difference is that the "spy" citizen of the country being betrayed may end up dead if they're caught, while the "spy" intelligence officer, who is probably a foreigner under cover as a "diplomat" will end up being thrown out of the country or jailed until they can be exchanged for another "spy" who has had his/her cover blown.

Recruitment

First you must "spot" a person who can be useful to your work. If I could rate some of the most desired people I would want to recruit as a spy, I would start with the keeper of the crown jewels. He might be the government minister who advises the leader of a country, or failing that, his secretary who knows where those jewels are kept and has access to a copying machine or a camera, or the general who writes the war plans, maybe his chief of staff who locks those plans up at night. Perhaps the scientist who invented the secret weapon or the assistant who knows what it looks like. Essentially, anyone who has access to something my country wants to know about.

I didn't mention the president or the prime minister, you say? I didn't, but on occasion one or two or those have been recruited, often when they were junior in rank or even before that when they were at school. You can never tell where a promising young student might end up.[32]

---

[31] Cambridge English Dictionary. https://dictionary.cambridge.org

[32] Sometimes you don't even need to recruit the agent, Lenin called those kind of people "useful idiots," people who are cynically manipulated by the another country to support a cause without understanding its consequences.

Another type of recruitment target is a support asset, someone that fulfills a specific duty like a courier, a safe-house keeper, a postal worker, or a member of a exfiltration network. All of these agents or assets need to be recruited with special vigilance to ensure the safety of those things with which they are to be entrusted.

MICE

In most instances, spies spy for one of several reasons and an oft stated acronym for that is MICE, which means money, ideology, compromise (blackmail), or ego — although money alone is rarely incentive enough. Revenge and the just plain thrill of the game factor in there. These are the approaches an intelligence officer might use to approach, assess, and recruit a spy.

Some recruiters will regale you with stories about the hard and dangerous work they've done to convince someone to become a traitor to their country or organization. In reality, it is often the "spy" who seeks out the recruiter to offer his services as a result of whatever motivation he or she might have. Veteran intel officers will admit that most all of the hard target recruitments done during the Cold War were volunteers. In other words, they were just looking for the opportunity to hand themselves and whatever they had to give over to the other side.

Once the spy has been recruited, what follows could be described as an illicit affair... secrecy, lies, excuses to your significant other that just don't make sense, furtive meetings in the night in the worst section of town, impossible demands levied by both parties, disappointment with the results, and either a break-up, discovery, or an escape.

The recruiter / case officer / handler must be a good judge of character and know how to handle his agent with respect and authority, but also have the ability to know when to use tact and compliments. If you can't deal with all kinds of people and personalities, the job isn't for you. One "case officer" told me he didn't like man-dating. He couldn't pretend to like someone just to get the access and information that was needed. He probably thought the work would be more like what he'd seen in the movies. As one would expect, his career in the field was rather short.

"I knew Rashid had picked up the dead drop when I got the message a few days later from an anonymous number saying my item was ready. We were scheduled to meet at a godforsaken patch of land Rashid had chosen at our last meeting.... I'd never before allowed him to choose the meeting location, but he'd kicked up such a fuss over the last site that I'd decided to throw him a bone, make him feel coddled and appreciated."
— *The Peacock and The Sparrow*, I.S.Berry.

Agent Handling

The handling of an agent is almost more important than recruitment because if the agent won't follow direction or can't be motivated, then he or she may be useless. A very few agents will shun any contact with their handler, but most need guidance and occasionally personal contact. Spying is a lonely business and reassurance that someone is there to help is often necessary. Part of the job description for a Case Officer is that they must continually assess their agents and plan how to motivate them as well as how to employ (use) them;

What follows is an extract from an agent operations plan (a West Berlin police officer) written by his MfS (Stasi) handler in the early 1960s. The agent was a volunteer and enthusiastic about his clandestine activities but needed to be directed into positions where he could satisfy the intelligence requirements of the agency:

Geheime Verschlußsache (**secret document**)

Berlin, den 26. Januar 1957

Perspectivplan (**operations plan**)

Possible uses of the Agent

The Agent has been a member of the West Berlin police since 1950. He has been a member of the Criminal Investigation Department since 1959. Before that, he worked for the police and mainly for the Operations Group. He was transferred to the Criminal Investigation Department on behalf of the MfS.

The Agent thus has the following access:

- Obtaining service instructions, orders, etc.

- Explaining the structure of the State Criminal Police Office - individual departments where the GM is deployed.

- Reporting on the training system of the West Berlin police - topic, content of the lessons, etc.

- Deployment on specific investigations for the MfS. (Investigations in residential areas, establishing personal details and car owners, etc.)

- Using connections through membership in the police shooting club. Some senior officers of the Schupo [uniformed Police] detachment also belong to this club — e.g. PHK Behrens - head of training for the FPR

Perspective of the Agent:

- The Agent is tasked with completing the preparatory course with good results. He must be among the selected candidates to attend the Hiltrupp school (police leadership school in Münster, FRG). After completion, the Agent will work as a middle cadre in the Criminal Investigation Department.

- The training of the Agent to improve and strictly adhere to the principles must be intensified. The focus must be on the GM's political education. (The training received in cipher and one-way radio must be reinforced by further training.) [handwritten note in the margin: "How? What?"]

- The Agent must make greater use of his personal connections with some officers of the police to obtain information. The GM must be trained more in this regard. [handwritten note in the margin: "more specific!"]

- The system of communication with the Agent must be improved. The possibilities for impersonal communication must be expanded. The GM is given the opportunity to use the material drop box at the Friedrichstrasse S-Bahn station.[33]

Signed: Chief of Department VII [34]   *Signed: Case Officer*

The agent described in the above document was one of *Stasi's* most important agents inside the West Berlin police force, providing information on personalities, operations, and warnings of investigations that might have compromised other agents and their handlers.

---

[33] Perspectivplan (Operational Goals), BStU, MfS, GH, Nr. 2/70, Bl. 213-214
[34] Department VII was the *Stasi* section responsible for intelligence on the West Berlin Police.

Illegals and Romeos (aka Honey Traps)

Stasi HVA (foreign intelligence) chief Markus Wolf's favorite MO was to send men and women up against vulnerable targets to began a romantic affair that could be exploited. Once the attachment was complete, the agent would entice his or her mate to provide sensitive materials. If the target was married, then coercion or blackmail might come into play. Often, love played its role and the target willingly supplied classified information in return for the agent's continued company.

The East Germans tended to go for its recruitments in West Germany…its capital city, Bonn, was the place for political recruitments, while Berlin was more about stealing the Allies' war plans. The Russians tried hard and succeeded at recruiting spies inside the military in Berlin and especially personnel who worked inside the electronic surveillance site at Teufelsberg to determine what the Allies knew about the Warsaw Pact from the extensive intercept capabilities that were centered there.

Berlin had more than its share of agent recruitments, many quite valuable and some of their stories are shared here.

Frau K — The Inside Woman

Frau K was a CIA asset in East Berlin. She was a housekeeper and worked inside the home of a Soviet KGB officer, Yevgeny Pitovranov when she came to the attention of the CIA's Berlin Operations Base. She was then hired by East German Military Intelligence Major General Karl Linke to take care of his home in the Karlshorst district of Berlin.

Prior to World War II, Linke had been a member of the communist party and escaped Germany to the USSR when Hitler came to power. After the war, he returned and took a position in the Barracked Peoples Police, the predecessor to the GDR's army, and rose through the ranks to become the East German chief of military intelligence. Fluent in German and Russian, he had close relations with Soviet military intelligence, the GRU, and access to many of their classified operations.

Linke and his wife were suspicious of Frau K from the beginning, perhaps because they were such fervent believers in the party, but despite that distrust, Frau K managed to copy documents that Linke carelessly left around his home office. In the summer of 1957, Frau K told her handler that she could not remain in the job because Linke's wife made her work unbearable. Further, Linke planned to go on leave for several months to his Dacha in the Soviet Union which would leave her with no work or pay for the summer.

Because of the high quality of her information, her BOB handler persuaded Frau K to stay in place for a few more months with the promise that she would be relocated and resettled in West Germany. Frau K reluctantly stayed but became alarmed when she accidentally marked a file with a pen while copying the document. Knowing she would be discovered, Frau K again pled to be extracted. After reviewing everything Frau K had brought with her, the BOB officers agreed. But they also knew that Linke would never be able to explain the security compromise so they came up with a plan to try and induce the general to defect. Frau K would make one more trip to the house to remove all the secret documents,

Typical KGB Officer
Apartment Block inside
the Karlshorst Compound
(credit: author)

including the one she had marked, and then leave an envelope for Linke that held 10,000 West Marks in cash and a forged West German passport in his name as enticement to defect. The BOB officers also gave her some wireless transmitters to be installed in the home which would allow BOB to gauge Linke's reaction to the letter. With only minor difficulties, Frau K was able to accomplish her tasks and escape to West Berlin.[35]

Nothing was heard from the transmitters and it was only later when Linke's deputy, Lieutenant Colonel Siegfried Dombrowski, defected that Linke's fate was learned. Dombrowski revealed that Linke was incensed by the housekeeper's treason and choose to show the letter to the *Stasi*.[36] Luckily for him the GDR government apparently decided to show some clemency by not executing him and instead demoted him to colonel and retired him from the military. He died in 1961. Frau K's true name has never been revealed but the information she managed to smuggle out revealed the level of Soviet subversive activities directed at the United States and the West German governments.[37]

---

[35] David E. Murphy; Kondrashev, Sergei A.; Bailey, George, Battle Ground Berlin, New Haven: Yale University Press, 1997.
[36] Klaus Behling, *Der Nachrichtendienst der NVA*, Berlin: Edition Ost, 2005, and Reinhard Gehlen, *The Service: The Memoirs of General Reinhard Gehlen*, Winter Park: World Publications, 1972.
[37] Murphy, Kandrashev, Bailey; *Battleground Berlin*.

McDonald's #1
(credit: author)

"Mister Gruen"

Hardcore "spotters" were worth their weight in gold in those days and still are... and "Mister Gruen" was one of the best.

A case told by Counterintelligence Officer Richard Gordon[38] is this one which shows a typical pattern the Soviets/Russians used against Americans in West Berlin. Somewhere mid or late 85...Gordon, a former Special Forces non-com who had switched to the counter-intelligence field when his age started to show, conducted reviews of soldiers to "bring-up" or renew their security clearances, a process conducted every couple of years. He along with another CI officer had developed a set of questions that went beyond the basics and were based on actual KGB/GRU/MfS recruitment approaches.

A lot depended on the personal interview side of the review because it provided an opportunity for an investigator to see and judge the soldier's physical reactions and verbal responses to questions, not something you can do with a written questionnaire. For one, Gordon and his colleague had been trained by the German Defense Ministry's Counter-intelligence Service (MAD), an organization that had extensive experience with Warsaw Pact espionage. One of the traits the Soviets and East German capitalized on was the fact that many U.S. senior NCOs and officers were into collecting stamps, small model trains, old coins, Nazi mementos and the like. Many soldiers bought souvenirs and collectibles in the East for hard DM under the table and brought them back into West Berlin. These things were also MfS/GRU standard forms of agent payments...as they knew the American authorities rarely asked about it. The Stasi/GRU/KGB knew U.S. soldiers and civilians responded to money most of the time. A second weakness was the inability of many soldiers to control their finances. This type of approach will appear again in another case, but often telephone calls were listened into and when a weakness was discovered, suddenly, a solution would appear in the form of a loan or financial specialist "cold-

---

[38] "Richard Gordon" is an alias as the GRU still nurses a serious grudge against him.

calling" the targeted soldier to help them out. Once spotted, the targeted soldier would be groomed for recruitment on the basis of his monetary needs.

One soldier called "Brad," who held a Top Secret clearance was being interviewed for an update when Gordon asked him if he'd been approached by anyone selling insurance. He had, the soldier said, and laid out the details. Mister Gruen met him initially at the most popular restaurant near the American housing quarter — the new McDonald's, the first one to open in Berlin and great place for an initial non-threatening meeting. Then they continued to meet at his apartment.

Mister Gruen worked several weeks with him doing a complete financial workup as to what he needed for his future — all debts, amounts earned, what his wife was earning and what his monthly needs were; everything needed to work out a financial plan. Brad had introduced Mister Gruen to about 15 other soldiers and now Gruen was doing their financial workups as well. They were all satisfied with his work, never giving the financial approach a single thought, feeling totally safe because Gruen was a UK citizen and also had a Portuguese passport and wife as well....and drove a nice Mercedes-Benz sports car.

Gordon asked his superiors to run traces on Gruen but they had reservations, for one, Gruen was not an American citizen and Gordon was told to lay off. Luckily, he was stubborn. Gordon took his suspicions to the British. He knew a liaison officer from SIS, and asked for their help to verify Gruen's history. They did, indicating he was a German-speaking Jewish refugee before the war and then joined the British Army and served as an interpreter in Germany. And yes, he had married a Portuguese wife and was residing in Portugal. They were also a bit suspicious and asked the German police to do a background check which resulted in more interesting information. Gruen had been a member of the German Communist Youth movement and had fled Germany in 1931...knowing that the Communists had sent many of their key youth out in the early 30s, information he left off his military entrance forms. But the Germans couldn't touch Gruen inside Berlin due to the rules of the Allied occupation.

Gordon went to his supervisors, but once again they had no interest. Then Gordon took his worries to the Germans directly, a MAD (counter-intel service) colonel who listened with interest. The colonel asked Gordon if he fully understood what he was describing. Gordon affirmed that he did and all the names and bio data went across the table. Four months later, Mister Gruen was arrested while he travelled in West Germany.[39] He was determined to have been one of the oldest and deepest moles in Europe. When Gruen's apartment was searched, he had over 13 different ID cards, one indicating he was an American civilian employee, and four different names. He spoke fluent German and Russian. He often travelled in the East with tourist groups. Tour operators knew only that he would "disappear and then reappear" at the crossing point and they never said anything because they assumed he was just shopping on his own.

Gruen was one of the best. In fact, he was a hardcore GRU officer — a colonel and had been working undercover since 1931 when he "fled" to England, until his arrest in 1986 — over 55 years in the business.

What did the Americans do about the other 15 soldiers? Nothing, they just moved on.....back to business as usual.[40]

---

[39] The West German MAD had no authority to arrest in West Berlin during the Cold War because of the city's status as an occupied city — at least until reunification.

[40] Richard Gordan (pseudonym), interview, 18 August 2016.

"Objekt Haus" - a typical East Berlin apartment block (credit: author)

USAF Sergeant Jeffrey Martin Carney aka "Uwe"

The strange case of the "Kid" is perhaps one of the saddest cases of espionage from the Cold War. It starts in 1983, when a young, naive American airman named Jeffery Carney decided he would try to save the world from the nuclear Apocalypse he thought was coming.[41]

Stationed in Berlin as a radio intercept specialist, Carney was fluent in German and had an incredible phonetic memory — that is, he could hear a voice once and then repeatedly identify to whom it belonged. In this case, it was the voices of the East German pilots he was monitoring.

As a member of the U.S. Air Force's 6912th Electronics Security Group at Tempelhof Central Airport, Carney had access to classified information of the highest level. Beside U.S. and NATO information, he understood the weaknesses of the Soviet and Warsaw Pact communications system.

---

[41] Lee E. Taylor II, "Counterintelligence Assessment of Jeffrey M. Carney, U.S. Air Force," Clifton, VA: American Intelligence Journal, Vol. 37, No. 1, 2020.

With the available information he saw, Carney felt that the United States was provoking the USSR into a war. This was at the time when a NATO exercise called "ABLE ARCHER 83" had the military leadership in Moscow believing war was imminent. For those and several personal reasons, Carney decided he would defect to East Germany. First, he hated his supervisors and believed them to be either stupid or warmongers. Second, he was gay and scared of being discovered. The complete circumstances are unclear, but he presented himself to the East German authorities at Checkpoint Charlie late on April 22, 1983, and requested asylum.

Stasi officers interviewed Carney and correctly assessed him to be vulnerable. His *Stasi* file stated simply that he was not motivated by anything "other than fear of legal punishment or lynching by his superiors." He lacked socialist tendencies. He was given an ultimatum: "Go back and spy for us or we will reveal the fact that you tried to defect."

He did and began spying, visiting the East several times and ultimately compromising hundreds of Top Secret programs including the complete file of a project called "Canopy Wing," which detailed vulnerabilities in the Soviet General Staff communications and a plan to infect Warsaw Pact systems with false and confusing orders. Code-named "Uwe" or "Kid," he worked for the East Germans directly (he loved Germany not the Soviet Union).

He was transferred back to the United States to Goodfellow Air Force Base where he taught German and bided his time until he could return to Germany. But the situation became risky, American counter-intelligence agents were ferreting out the Soviet Union's spies all over the country and Carney, who also feared that his sexual orientation would be discovered, panicked. In 1985, he fled to Mexico City and showed up on the doorstep of the East German Embassy demanding to be taken "home." Seeing a use for Carney, they acquiesced to his demands and flew him to East Berlin by way of Havana.

Once back in Berlin, he served the *Stasi* as a translator, eavesdropping on U.S. military commanders and the American Embassy. He was given a new identity as Jens Karney with an East German passport and an apartment on Pintschstrasse in East Berlin. At another safe spot called "Objekt Brücke" located at Köpenicker Staße 114, he translated surveillance tapes he was provided for 8 hours a day. He was paid 1,400 Ostmarks per month and given a 1,500 Deutsch-Marks bonus every year. He also received two medals from his hosts.

Then, in late 1989, his world fell apart. With the fall of the Berlin Wall and the dissolution of East Germany, the Stasi files on the spies they were handling came to the attention of the West German Office of the Protection of the Constitution (BfV) and then the CIA.[42] Among those files was Jeffery Carney's and he quickly became a target. The information was turned over to the USAF Office of Special Investigations and Carney/Karney was tracked down. In April 1991, the OSI succeeded in locating his apartment — probably with the help of a recently unemployed *Stasi* officer — and arrested him. He was quickly returned to the United States and debriefed. With a pre-trial agreement, Carney pled guilty to the charges of espionage, conspiracy and desertion in exchange for a 25-year sentence. He was released after 12 years. Since then, he has tried to return to Germany claiming he was a citizen of the former East.

Unfortunately for him, the Federal Republic of Germany does not recognize his expired passport as proof of citizenship. It seemed nobody loved him anymore.

---

[42] More probably it happened the other way around; the CIA may have acquired the files first. See the "Rosewood Files" later in this book.

Eierschale logo
(credit: Eierschale)

Romeo and Juliet

Berlin's *Eierschale* (Eggshell) bar was a favorite place not only for its music but also for espionage approaches as a lot of "available" men and women were on the prowl most evenings and during weekend afternoon brunches where as much jazz as beer was on tap. Close to the American military headquarters on Clayallee it was a great location to zero-in on a potential recruitment target. I'm disappointed because I went there a number of times and never got approached. In any event, a sanitized version of one such encounter follows:

"Juliet" met her Romeo in July 1977 on the banks of the Spree River following a night at the bar. It was love at first sight for the divorcee. "Romeo" was seven years her senior and under cover as a scientist employed by a research company who travelled extensively — or so he told her. The couple became engaged three months after meeting. Juliet worked as a translator and interpreter at the American Consulate. She met her Romeo once a month and passed him thousands of official documents. She was madly in love with him and never questioned him about what he did with the information she gave him. But then he disappeared just after the Berlin Wall fell in 1990. A year later, she was betrayed by files an investigator found while searching through the seized Stasi archives. Juliet went on trial for espionage. During the trial, she focused solely on finding out as much as she could about her true love, trying to determine if really loved her. She was given a two-year suspended sentence and fined. The presiding judge concluded her "blind adoration" for her Romeo had led her to spy. She never found her true love.43

— The *Eierschale* is located at Landhaus Dahlem, Podbielskiallee 50.

---

43 CIA, *Romeo Spies,* https://www.cia.gov/stories/story/romeo-spies/, article retrieved June 2018.

Meister, the Turkish Mechanic and the American Traitor

Sometimes it takes a traitor to find a traitor.

This story begins when an East Berliner was arrested for shoplifting inside the massive KaDeWe department store in West Berlin. When the West Berlin Polizei interrogated him, the man revealed he was a citizen of East Berlin. It was unusual that a commoner would be able to travel to the West freely, after all, that privilege was reserved for diplomats or high functionaries in the communist government, and folks over 65. Or spies. The man was a language lecturer at the Humboldt University in East Berlin, not a position that would normally afford him the opportunity to travel.[44]

Because of that the police suspected he might be a *Stasi* employee. When they asked, he immediately confirmed that he was a support asset but insisted he didn't spy on West Germany; he was a low-level support asset for operations directed against the Americans. The Germans quickly brought the CIA into the case and they decided he was a "small fish" and a better fit for U.S. Army Counterintelligence. The man then insisted he wanted a deal and offered the little secret info he knew in exchange for relocation to the West with his family. The Americans, however, wanted better information so they gave him a contact number and let him return to East Berlin until he had something better.

A couple of years passed before he contacted his handler again. He was met and debriefed again inside West Berlin. This time he asserted that he was an interpreter at a *Stasi* meeting with an American soldier who was providing stolen intelligence, the officers' ears perked up. The soldier, code-named "Paul," was a signals intercept specialist and had been paid handsomely for his treachery, to the tune of at least $30,000 U.S. Dollars. He described Paul's appearance, mentioned that the Stasi interviewers had twice called him "James," and that he was married to a West German woman. According to Karl's rapid fire description, the American soldier also served in Berlin at the Teufelsberg intercept site and had been reassigned back to the United States. When he told the Americans that "Paul" had shared code-word information on two highly-classified programs they knew they had a big case on their hands.[45]

A bit of research in the records was needed but it didn't take long for the investigators to identify the soldier as James W. Hall. They couldn't arrest him, at least not until they had proof that Hall had sold secrets to the enemy. Without that, the suspect couldn't be indicted. There was another problem. The East German source who revealed the spy was still in East Berlin. If Hall was arrested, it was likely he would be compromised and probably executed. A plan was necessary.

An extensive surveillance program was launched to cover James Hall's activities. He was now stationed at Fort Stewart, Georgia and the investigators put into place physical and technical surveillance measures while they also scoured the man's financial records. They had to be careful so that Hall wasn't tipped off. If he had been, he would have undoubtably made a run for the border to escape arrest.[46]

About the same time, a curious thing happened. Hall's mother received a call at her home in New York from a man who asked to have her son call him in Florida. The surveillance team heard the conversation and were then surprised to hear Hall call the number and ask for a man whose name was already well known to several of the investigators, Huseyin Yildirim. A Turkish guest worker in West Berlin, Yildirim's name had come up during an investigation years before. He had

---

[44] His true name was Manfred Severin.
[45] Herrington, COL Stuart A., *Traitors Among Us,* San Diego: Harcourt-Harvest, 1999.
[46] Stephen Engelberg, Michael Wines, "U.S. Says Soldier Crippled Spy Post Set Up in Berlin," NY: *New York Times, May 7, 1989.*

been employed by the U.S. Army as an auto mechanic where he was called *"Meister"* and also taught car repair and restoration to soldiers on their free time at the Auto Craft Shop on Andrews Barracks. He had once been accused of soliciting information from soldiers, but the investigation was closed without resolution. He married an American and moved to the United States where he had settled in Florida.[47]

Yildirim's appearance in the States was a surprise for the investigators and they immediately surmised that he could be a contact man in the United States for the *Stasi*. They had no idea that he had been in contact with Hall before the telephone call. With this new twist in the case, the FBI began covering Yildirim and the Army continued watching Hall. A series of events connected the two men — they met furtively several times at highway rest stops and restaurants. Hall received some documents from Yildirim at a restaurant and the pass was photographed, but there was still no evidence of Hall giving anything to the contact. Finally, Hall was caught on camera taking some secret information home from his office.

As the investigators had been warned not to permit Hall to turn over any more classified material, they suspected they had little time before they would have to act and the pressure increased to resolve the case before Hall figured out he was being watched and tried to flee. A new element was introduced to speed up the process. The East German volunteer who had given Hall up, was exfiltrated out of East Berlin and brought to the United States to do one more job. He would be put to use reprising his Stasi role to cold call Hall and ask for a meeting at a motel. The story was that Hall was being turned over from the *Stasi* to the KGB for continued handling. The volunteer didn't introduce Hall to a KGB officer but to a FBI Special Agent who was posing as one.[48]

Once in the motel room, things progressed quickly. Using the information the interpreter provided, the FBI Agent quickly "established" the relationship getting Hall to accept more money and admit his treason. He also provided enough information to definitively establish that Yildirim had enabled his first contact with the *Stasi* in Berlin. With the meeting over, Hall left the room and was promptly arrested.

Hall's treason, however, didn't start with the *Stasi*. It started with the KGB with whom he'd already made contact and was providing secrets. Then, Hall happened to be at the U.S. Army's Auto Crafts Shop where Yildirim worked and jokingly mentioned that he needed to find a way to earn even more money. Yildirim himself was already an "purveyor of secrets" who had been selling information to the East Germans and was able to persuade Hall to provide more secrets, ostensibly for his friends in the Turkish government. Hall had no problem with that and before long he was playing both the Russians and East Germans by selling the same information twice. Yildirim was arrested at almost the same moment as Hall and, even though he was faced with the evidence, he denied his role as a spy. Both men received long prison sentences.[49]

[47] Bernd von Kostka, "The Turkish Spy Handler: Hüseyin Yildirim," https://www.casemateuk.com/blog/2021/11/09/the-turkish-spy-handler-huseyin-yildirim/

[48] David Wise, "The FBI's Fake Russian Agent Reveals His Secrets," Washington DC: The Smithsonian, 2016.

[49] DHRA, "JAMES HALL III," Biographical Entry, https://www.dhra.mil/PERSEREC/Espionage-Cases/army1/, retrieved April 2024.

MfS *"Stasi"* Identification Book, ID Disc, and Weapons Receipts (author's collection)

Werner Stiller MfS - "Bring him back or render him harmless. Now."

Spies are recruited to betray their country. Sometimes they are spotted and recruited by an intelligence officer (IO) who asks them to provide secret or privileged information, but often they recruit themselves. The IO just gives the would-be spy a convenient opportunity to act on what they have already decided.

Werner Stiller recruited himself. He was educated as a physicist and was then recruited by the Ministry of State Security to work in HA II, the *Stasi's* scientific-technical espionage department. As an intelligence officer, he recruited agents who gave him information on microprocessing, nuclear weapons technology and other scientific subjects that would help the GDR's economy and its military.[50]

Increasingly at odds with the repressive methods of the East German regime and his employer, he decided one day that he'd had enough. "The system became repugnant to me," he later said. That was one part of the story. The other part was that his career had stagnated and he'd been counseled by a superiors over an affair with a woman. That same woman helped Stiller to get to get an encrypted message to Pullach, the Federal German intelligence service (BND) headquarters near Munich,

---

[50] BStU, "Sachstandsbericht über die Ereignisse nach der Flucht Werner Stillers," BStU, MfS, HA II, Nr. 36560, Bl. 292-298.

offering his services and, for at least five months, he received instructions from the West and answered them with letters that included secret messages written with invisible ink.

One of Stiller's letters was discovered by the East German postal inspectors (which had its own special department inside the MfS). Although the investigators were not yet able to identify its origin, Stiller knew it was time to leave when he discovered the letter had been intercepted. In the early evening of January 18, 1979, he returned to his office and grabbed a thick file of microfiche documents — by some accounts 20,000 pages of classified files — along with a forged travel order, and headed for the border. He left his family behind having said good-bye and left a letter to his wife with 10,000 West German Marks inside.[51]

The system for crossing the border was well known to Stiller. He was responsible for handling at least 30 agents in the West and traveled there often enough to know the drill. With a forged transit permission document in hand, he went not to the regular border crossing at Friedrichstraße's so-called "Palace of Tears," but a small building around back. This side entrance was what the Stasi Department XXVII called an *Operative Grenzschleusen,* or operational barrier crossing. It was at locations like these that Stasi operatives and sometimes their spies could slip across the intercity border (the Wall) or even the frontier with West Germany without the controls everyone else had to endure.[52]

Stiller had used this portal several times before but in his haste had overlooked a mistake in his papers. He blamed his secretary and hoped the man wouldn't call his supervisors to confirm the trip was valid. The man, who knew Stiller, finally acquiesced and permitted him "this one time" to pass through the barrier. Stiller hopped on the U-Bahn subway rather than the overhead S-Bahn which he knew to be better controlled. He didn't want to meet any more of his colleagues. He crossed into West Berlin and proceeded to Tegel Airport where he turned himself into the police. Since the West Germans were not permitted to fly a military plane into Berlin, they turned him over to the Americans who flew him out the next day from Tempelhof Airfield to Munich where he underwent a year of debriefings by the BND.

Stiller's defection was a major slap in the face to his former employer. Erich Mielke, the MfS chief gave the order to find him and bring him back and if that wasn't possible " render him harmless." It was a death sentence that would never be carried out.[53]

Stiller's information blew the covers of a lot of Stasi agents in West Germany, at least 17 were convicted and imprisoned while another 15 or so were forced to escape back to the East. For this, Stiller was paid 400,000 West Marks and given a new identity as Klaus Peter Fischer. Thereafter, he moved to the United States where the CIA also debriefed him and used his *Stasi* tradecraft information to teach new officers. When he was finished, the Agency arranged for him attend university to learn about business, which he leveraged into a lucrative career as a stockbroker for several high-powered Wall Street firms. The communist Stiller had done a full U-turn and became Klaus-Peter Fischer, the capitalist. When the Berlin Wall fell, he moved back to Germany for a while but couldn't come to terms with life in a reunified Germany. He passed away in Budapest in 2016.

---

[51] BStU, "Bildbericht zum Diebstahl von geheimen Unterlagen durch Werner Stiller," MfS, HA IX, Nr. 24336, Bl. 108-119

[52] *"Unsichtbare Löcher in der Mauer" (Invisible Holes in the Wall),* Bundes Archive, https://www.bundesarchiv.de/themen-entdecken/online-entdecken/storys/grenzschleusen/, retrieved 18 September 2024.

[53] BStU, Schreiben Erich Mielkes über den Umgang mit Verrätern aus den eigenen Reihen, BStU, MfS, BdL/Dok., Nr. 6908, Bd. 10, Bl. 1-8.

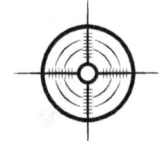

CHAPTER VII
»Horch und Guck«

Operation Gold / Stopwatch: the Berlin Tunnel

Not all of Berlin's secret tunnels were dug to escape from East Berlin to the West. Probably the most famous Cold War tunnel was dug under the intercity border by the CIA and SIS to tap into and eavesdrop on Soviet and East German communications. The tunnel was in operation from March 1955 until April 1956, when it was discovered by the Soviets. Although it was compromised from the beginning by the British spy George Blake, it did provide critical military intelligence, along with classified information about Soviet atomic research and development.[54]

Precursor

The idea for Operation Gold / Stopwatch came partially from another, much smaller, surveillance project called Operation Silver, a British program that tapped into the Soviet Army headquarters landline communications in Vienna, Austria from 1949 to 1955. OP Silver was never discovered and ended only when Austria regained full sovereignty. The British monitoring station was disguised as a clothing shop. It was only in 1951, when the CIA divulged their plan to tap into Russian communications in Berlin to the SIS, that the SIS revealed their own operation in Vienna.[55]

The Operation

Code-named "Operation Gold" by the CIA and "Stopwatch" by SIS, the project was intended to capture intelligence from telecommunications cables in the Soviet sector of East Berlin. The CIA and SIS agreed to run the operation jointly, although the Americans would do most of the construction (British specialists would assist).[56] The operation began in 1951, but it took two years to determine the best place to dig the tunnel, final approval was received in January 1954.

---

[54] Blake, a SIS officer, was captured in Korea and "turned" to become a double agent when he returned to the UK in 1953.

[55] Blake also revealed Operation Silver to the KGB in 1953, but it had already been shut down.

[56] SIS codenamed their participation in the project as Operation Stopwatch.

Aerial photo of the Op Gold/Stopwatch tunnel route into East Berlin (credit: Allierten Museum Berlin / U.S. Air Force - Chodan)

Recovered and Reconstructed Gold / Stopwatch Tunnel at Allied Museum (credit: author)

The exact site to tap into the cables was determined by CIA-recruited East German agents within the East German Ministry of Post and Telecommunications, including one who worked in the long-distance department who was able to provide directories of cable users. Another asset provided engineering diagrams and maps of Soviet cable lines inside Berlin. The specific site was chosen in the southern part of the city called Berlin-Altglienicke where a junction existed for cables that ran under the street (Schönefelder Chaussee) and which connected the Soviet Army's communications lines between Moscow and the Group of Soviet Forces in Germany (GSFG) in Wünsdorf.

Tunnel construction began early in 1954. A specially designed warehouse was built in the southern Berlin district of Rudow just inside the American sector. Ostensibly, or perhaps ironically, the site was disguised as a U.S. Army electronic collection station complete with working antennas. The warehouse was built by a German contractor with an extraordinarily deep basement to allow for the soil that was to be removed from the tunnel and ramps that — according to the cover story —were for forklifts to be used in a new and improved quartermaster storage facility. Once the warehouse was completed, secret tunneling began in August with the work being carried out by the U.S. Army Corps of Engineers. When completed it was 1,476 feet in length; 3,100 tons of soil were removed (and stored in the basement); with 125 tons of steel liner plate installed. Extraordinary engineering procedures had to be used because the tunnel could not be dug too deep as the water table was high, nor could it be too close to the surface to guard against discovery. To eliminate traces of the digging, washing machines were installed in the warehouse to clean the workers clothing. No trace of the operation could be deduced from outside observation of the site.

Once the tunnel reached the Schönefelder Chaussee, a vertical shaft was dug to the target cables. British specialists made the first taps into the cables in May 1955. The telephone and signal cables were

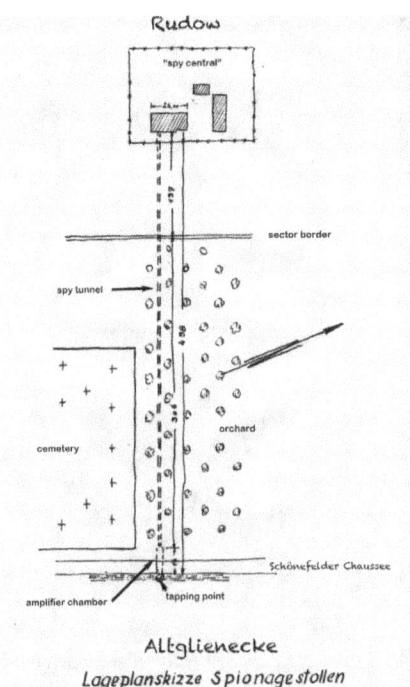

Rudow

"spy central"

sector border

spy tunnel →

cemetery

orchard

Schönefelder Chaussee

amplifier chamber   tapping point

Altglienecke

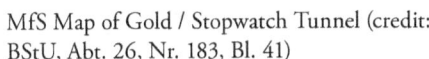
Lageplanskizze Spionagestollen

MfS Map of Gold / Stopwatch Tunnel (credit: BStU, Abt. 26, Nr. 183, Bl. 41)

A Soviet officer reads the English labels of the equipment inside the tunnel. (credit: BA, Bild 183-37695-0003 / Junge, Peter Heinz / CC-BY-SA 3.0 VII.4)

connected to an array of amplifiers and tape recording machines that were mounted inside the tunnel behind a reinforced steel door that would provide an extra measure of security and importantly, a bit more time if the tap chamber was somehow discovered. As a last measure of security, a warning sign in Russian and German was hung on the door from the tap chamber into the tunnel that said "Do Not Enter by Order of the Soviet Commandant"

Once operations began, the raw recordings were sent to the United Kingdom and then the United States for processing and analysis.

The fly in the ointment was that the KGB was already aware of Operation Gold through George Blake, a double agent for the Soviets who joined SIS in 1953. Blake, who was employed in a technical section, took part in a briefing on the operation and provided the information to his Soviet handler. Because Blake was a valuable asset, the KGB decided not to compromise the tunnel in order to protect him. The KGB did not inform anyone of their knowledge and neither the Soviet Army commander in East Germany nor the East Germans themselves were given any notice. Only the highest echelons of the KGB were aware and they chose to permit the uncensored, unfettered flow of information rather than give up their prize asset.

It was only when Blake was transferred that the Soviets could move against the tunnel. In 1956, the Soviet Union staged a 'discovery' using a pretext of tracing water leaks that were said to be damaging subterranean phone lines. On April 23, 1956, the acting military commander of the Soviet sector of Berlin, Colonel Kozjuba, announced the discovery at a press conference, saying they had surprised American technicians sipping their coffee by their recording machines.

The Americans had a different story. On the night of April 22, observers at the warehouse saw soldiers digging holes along the Schönefelder Chaussee and warned the technicians of a possible

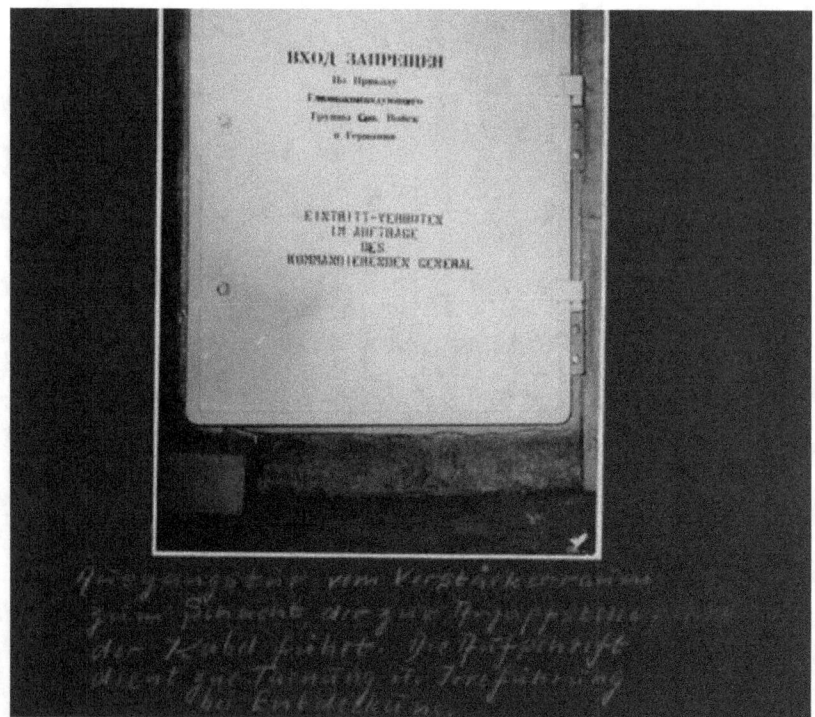

Do Not Enter by Order of the Soviet Commandant (credit: BStU, MfS, ZAIG, Fo, Nr. 2815, Bl. 6)

intrusion, giving them time to retreat behind the steel door. That said, the cable was cut and the project ended in a propaganda coup for Soviet Premier Nikita Khruschchev. He used the incident to denounce the Americans but because he was about to visit the UK, he choose to blame the Americans alone.[57]

After George Blake's arrest in 1961 and the discovery of the depths of his treachery, the Berlin Tunnel was declared a failure. Many considered the information collected to have been a deception operation, all the information being contrived by the KGB to fool the Americans and British.

Details revealed since 1990 indicate, however, that the tunnel was actually successful. The "take" was at least 50,000 reels of tape with some 368,000 Soviet and 75,000 East German conversations, resulting in around 1,750 intelligence reports. It would have been impossible for the Soviets to fake that much information or that many telephone calls. Besides revealing the latest developments in Soviet atomic research, the tapes showed disagreements between the Soviets and the East Germans over the status of West Berlin, as well as information on the 20th Party Congress in the USSR.

Today

Little evidence of the tunnel exists today. The tunnel was excavated by the East Germans on their side of the Wall in the late 1950s and a section of it was discovered during the construction of the Autobahn A113 in 2008. Another excavated section has been restored as a display inside the Allied Museum Berlin.

— *Allierten Museum Berlin* (currently at Clayallee 135, but soon moving to Tempelhof Airfield), U-Bahnhof Oskar-Helene-Heim (U3), Bus Stop AlliiertenMuseum, 115 or X83.

---

[57] Or perhaps, he was trying divert attention from their mole George Blake. Much of the recording and amplification equipment used in the operation was of British manufacture.

RIAS *Stasi* surveillance photo (credit BA, MfS, ZAIG, Nr. 9961, Teil 1, Bl. 116)

RIAS — Cold War on the Airwaves

"Hier ist RIAS Berlin – eine freie Stimme der freien Welt."[58]

Rundfunk im amerikanischen Sektor or Radio in the American Sector (RIAS) played an important part throughout the Cold War.

Mistrust and suspicion abounded in post-war Berlin. Immediately after the cessation of hostilities, the Soviet Military Government set up a radio station in the old Nazi "Radio Berlin" and began transmitting information as well as pro-Russian propaganda. The Allies tried to gain access to the station but were refused.

As an independent counter to the Soviet-controlled broadcasts, the American military administration set up RIAS Berlin in 1946. It advertised itself as "the free voice of the free world," and served as a broadcasting bridge to the West for citizens of the GDR. First as "Drahtfunk *im amerikanischen Sektor*" or wired radio, then as an 800-watt radio transmitter that could not cover the entire city, Radio In the American Sector came into being on 5 September 1946 with music and shortly thereafter with the RIAS Symphony Orchestra that played, ironically enough in Hitler's capital, music of Jewish composers who had been banned during the Nazi years. More importantly, American jazz and "rock and roll" began to be played at night.

The most important contribution of RIAS to Berlin and before long, East Germany was its news, read aloud by native German speakers. Although the supervision of RIAS Berlin broadcasting and programming was in the hands of the United States Information Service, much of the content

---

[58] "Here is RIAS Berlin - A Free Voice of the Free World" - the Station's slogan.

RIAS / Deutschland Radio Today (credit: Avda CCA3)

was determined by it employees.[59] By 1950, RIAS was broadcasting children's programs and even a teaching program called *"Schulfunk"* or school radio. It also provided complete and impartial reporting on political developments within the city, while the Soviet-controlled Radio Berlin only transmitted news about SED politics.

The East German government realized that RIAS would be one of its biggest problems as more and more of the populace tuned in. Calling it a *"Hetzsender"* or hate broadcaster it claimed:

"The RIAS is one of the agent centers in West Berlin which, like it and closely intertwined with it and with each other, are trying to disguise their crimes against the German nation with the most sophisticated means."— *DDR-Generalstaatsanwalts* (GDR attorney general).

RIAS broadcast programs reported on events within the Soviet Zone, stories that were usually censored in the East and, further, it openly called for improvements in work norms for all East German workers based on reporting from workers who had spoken with journalists.

When the workers' uprising of 17 June 1953 occurred in East Berlin, it was RIAS that kept up around-the-clock reporting of events and incidents as they unfolded. Some have surmised that without RIAS, the revolution would never have spread to the rest of the country. This event, more than any other, propelled the *MfS "Stasi"* to target RIAS in order to undermine its operations,

---

[59] Prof. Herbert Kundler, "RIAS Berlin and the Americans," RIAS Berlin Kommission, 2024, (on-line article https://riasberlin.org/en/history/articles/)

1952 GDR Propaganda Poster - "Broadcasting in American pay!" (credit: PD)

influence and dissuade its broadcasters, and determine where its information was coming from in order to arrest the sources.

In 1955, before the Wall was erected, the Stasi managed to insert a spy into the RIAS offices. The operation was code-named *Enten* (Ducks) and resulted in the arrest of 49 East Germans. The spy discovered their names in the radio station. They included ordinary people from all social classes who had contacted RIAS and provided it political news, economic information, reports on the mood in everyday life, and revelations about remilitarization in the GDR. At least one was executed, most served prison terms.[60]

The events of June 1953, and the later Hungarian Revolution in 1956, served to show the people of the East that the West would not intervene in their internal affairs, a position made clearer during the Berlin Crisis of 1961 and the construction of the Berlin Wall.

RIAS was shut down in 1992 and its facilities at the Funkhaus am Hans-Rosenthal-Platz turned into the station *Deutschland Radio Kultur,* a change that ended its status as "a free voice of the free world" and its contributions to the reunification of Germany. The RIAS sign still stands on the roof of the building and has received status as a protected monument *(Denkmalschutz).*

RIAS and its role in the "propaganda war" of the 1950s figures prominently and is accurately portrayed in Joseph Kanon's novel, *Leaving Berlin.*

— RIAS Funkhaus am Hans-Rosenthal-Platz, S-Bahnhof Innsbrucker Platz (S42, S46), U-Bahnhof Rathaus Schöneberg (U4)

---

[60] Karl Wilhelm Fricke, "Vor 50 Jahren: Stasi-Aktion „Enten"," Deutschlandradiofunk, (article on-line: https://www.deutschlandradio.de/unternehmen-106.html)

JAROC (B) — Receiving the Huddled Masses

Joint Allied Refugee Operations Center, Berlin operated under the authority of the U.S. Commander of Berlin's DCSI (Deputy Chief of Staff Intelligence).

JAROC's mission was to screen all refugee or emigré arrivals to West Berlin from Eastern European countries. All the arrivals would first be screened at the Marienfelde Refugee Center — a holding "camp" called *Marienfelde Notaufnahmelager* (emergency reception camp) in Germany. Here all three western allies participated in that process. Between 1949 to 1990, about four million people "voted with their feet" and left the GDR for the West. The Marienfelde reception center was the first point of contact in the West for 1.35 million of them.

Those that had no intelligence value were turned over to the German government for further processing. Those that might have intelligence information were further, but separately debriefed at three different Allied locations — Sven-Hedin 11 in Zehlendorf for the Americans, in Charlottenburg for the British, and Reinickendorf for the French.

The staff of the screening centers consisted mainly of civilian employees or members of various intelligence organizations. Many of the interviewers spoke several languages, but they were not allowed to have any family or connection to the Eastern Bloc and visiting the East was also prohibited. Almost all employees had code names for their own security.

Both the JAROC sites at Sven-Hedin Straße and Marienfelde were primary collection targets for Stasi intelligence officers. Of special interest to the Stasi was the questioning system and the associated activities of the western secret services with regard to the refugees. They wanted to determine if any of the refugees might be "turned" and enticed to return to the GDR as spies and also exactly what information the refugees might have revealed to the Allies.

— JAROC-B, Sven-Hedin 11 at Karl Hofer Strasse, U-Bahnhof Krumme Lanke (U3), S-Bahnhof Mexicoplatz (S2), Bus Stop Mexicoplatz (118, 622)

— Marienfelde Refugee Center Museum, S-Bahnhof Marienfelde (S2), Bus Stop Erinnerungsstätte Marienfelde (M77)

Stasi Surveillance Photo of JAROC-B Marienfelde Refugee Center (credit: BA, MfS, ZKG, Fo, Nr. 287, Bild 11)

JAROC-B
Headquarters
Sven-Hedin 11
(credit: author)

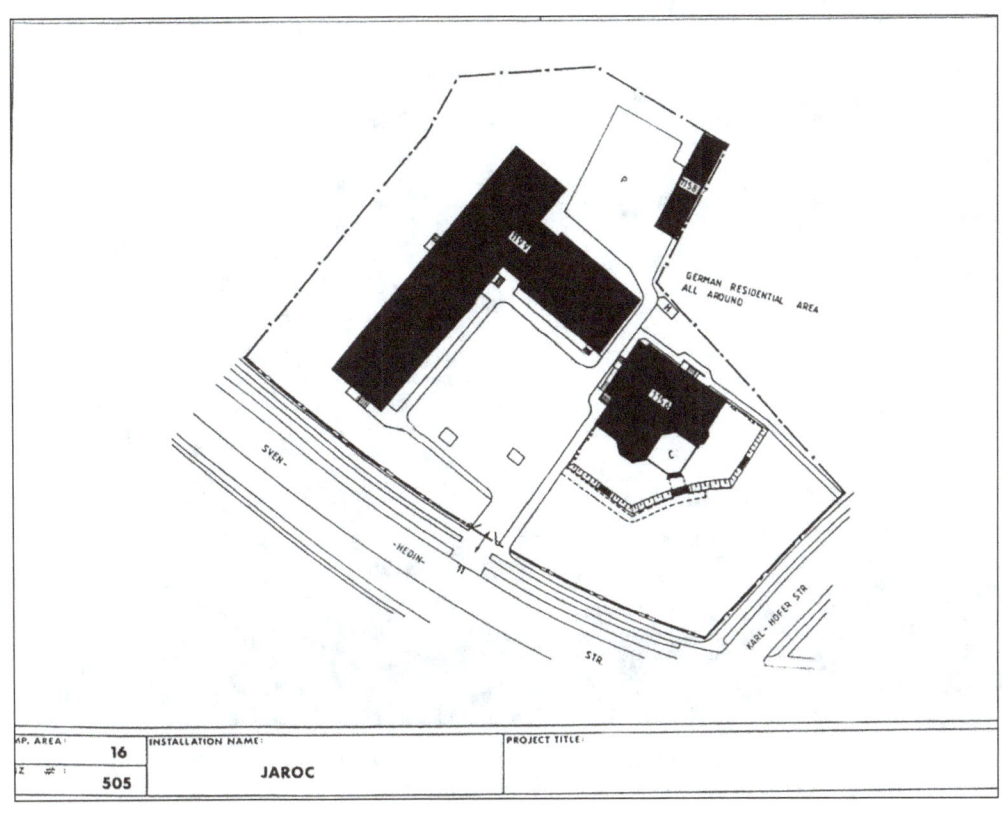

U.S. Army Map of
JAROC(B) (credit:
USCOB)

Palast Hotel

The Palast Hotel was opened in 1979 in the Berlin district of Mitte, directly on the Spree, bordered by Karl-Liebknecht-Strasse and Spandauer Strasse. On the other side of the river was the Berlin Cathedral and the Palace of the Republic, which has since also been demolished. The Marx-Engels Forum lay to the south across Karl-Liebknecht-Strasse.

Planning for a new hotel began in 1976 and construction work began shortly thereafter and when completed boasted 600 rooms and 40 suites with 1000 beds towered above. The Palast was one of several GDR hotels that could only be used by patrons with convertible currencies, i.e., West Marks or U.S. Dollars. It was intended for a western clientele with products that were otherwise not available in the East, such as limousines from BMW, Audi and Volvo.

The MfS monitored large parts of the hotel with hidden audio and video recording devices in around 30 special rooms for guests of special interest to the Stasi. The MfS used prostitutes to exploit certain westerner guests. The hotel was also used by special friends of the *Stasi*, including Abu Daoud, the terrorist mastermind of the Munich hostage-taking in 1972 and reportedly Ilich Ramírez Sánchez, aka "Carlos the Jackal."

After German reunification, the hotel continued to be operated by various companies until it was closed and demolished in 2001. The CityQuartier DomAquarée was built on its site, which now houses a hotel from the Radisson Collection chain.

— CityQuartier DomAquarée, Karl-Liebknecht-Straße 5

Palast Hotel in 1986 with the Dom Cathedral (credit: PD)

Palast Hotel and Bargepusher on the Spree in 1985 (credit: BA, Bild 183-1985-0415-029 / Junge, Peter Heinz / CC-BY-SA 3.0VII.13

Palast Hotel and Tourboat on the Spree in 2024 (credit: author)

Hotel Luftbrücke — Home for a Murder Cell

A Lebanese grill and a Shisa bar on the ground floor of a seedy apartment building are all that remains of one of the East German *MfS's* most unusual endeavors in West Berlin, a safe-house that turned a profit as a hotel.

That was the *Hotel Luftbrücke,* code-named *"Stützpunkt Rheinland"* in Stasi files. The "owners" were West Germans recruited as *"IMA"*[61] by the *Stasi Hauptabteilung VIII.*[62] That department was responsible for surveillance, investigation, search, and arrests for other sections of the MfS. HA VIII's targets were people or facilities, but an additional task was eliminating enemies of the State.

The two IMs began their work in 1974. IM "Karate" was a 40-year old wanted burglar who was introduced to the Stasi by another agent. The Stasi had no inhibitions about recruiting criminals for what was essentially contract work. His first assignment was nothing less than an assassination attempt on Siegfried Schulze, an opponent of the SED living in West Berlin. It failed, but Schulze was badly injured.

His partner was a young woman, IM "Janett." She had been part of a gang and later a striptease dancer in Frankfurt am Main. She was recruited by "Karate" and before long they were a team with their living expenses financed and bonus payments for jobs well done. They carried out assignments in West Germany and West Berlin, sometimes in other European countries, checking addresses, photographing people, and watching their target's daily routines.

Happy with "Karate" and his skills at breaking into buildings and stealing documents, the Stasi strove to create a comprehensive cover legend for both IMs. They needed a way to legitimize the pair with a business in West Berlin that "Janett" could run to demonstrate a legal income. So they bought a run-down hotel, the "Luftbrücke," right next to Tempelhof Airport. They gave the couple 95,000 DM for the lease and gave it the code name "Rheinland." The new proprietor, "Janett," turned the hotel into a profitable business over the next five years. The US Air Force was a regular customer and the information on the hotel guests was an interesting by-product. For her work, "Janett" was awarded a medal: "In recognition of many years of loyal service. — National People's Army."

Karate trained for more sensitive missions: surveillance and eavesdropping, and was given more equipment for special tasks. His file reads:

"The IM is equipped with operational technology:

- Car – can also be used as a covered surveillance post,

- Photo equipment,

- Radio equipment,

- Documents (fake passports) provided,

- Training in clandestine entry,

- Theoretical and practical shooting exercises."[63]

---

61 *Inoffizieller Mitarbeiter mit besonderen Aufgaben - Unofficial collaborator with special tasks.*

62 Main Department VIII.

63 Konstanze Soch, with Gabriele Camphausen, Stasi in Berlin: *Die DDR-Geheimpolizei in der geteilten Stadt,* Berlin: BStU, 2022.

Stasi Surveillance Photo of the Luftbrücke Hotel (credit: MfS, AIM 9229/87, Bd. 2, Bl. 237)

"Luftbrücke" Dudenstraße 6 in 2024 (credit: author)

The Stasi judged that its goal of creating a viable cover for the two IM was fully achieved in 1981, but when the five-year lease expired, the hotel was given up because of its expected high renovation costs. Despite an illness that prevented "Janett" from working regularly and "Karate" continued working in West Germany. "Karate" was again involved in a Stasi operation called *"Parasit"* against *"Fluchthelfer"* (escape helper) Julius Lamp'l. "Karate" was supposed to attach a bomb to Lamp'l's car. Luckily for Lamp'l, the operation didn't happen.[64]

The West German authorities had stepped up their search for "Karate." The Stasi moved him to East Berlin in 1983, gave him a new identity and an apartment. "Janett" separated from him and, after recovering from her illness, continued to carry out Stasi assignments in West Germany until 1986.

After the Wall came down, "Karate" lost his allowances. He was arrested in 1992 and charged with attempted murder. In all, HA VIII is thought to have been responsible for 500 contract murders in West Germany.

— Hotel Luftbrücke, Dudenstraße 6.

---

[64] "Fluchthelfer" were anyone who helped GDR citizens to escape and were considered "Enemies of the State."

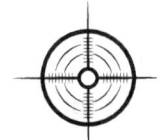

CHAPTER VIII
Active Measures & Terrorists

**"Not a single agent of war-mongering imperialism will be safe, wherever he hangs out –
be it West Berlin, Bonn, Paris or even Washington."** — *Neues Deutschland,* the East German
Socialist Unity Party (SED) official newspaper

Following World War II, the Western Allies were concerned with finding war criminals, unlike
the security services of the Eastern Bloc who were occupied with locating, neutralizing, and in
many cases eliminating anyone perceived to threaten the communist regime. Three methods have
been favored to take care of such business, none of them are new: Defenestration, Liquidation,
Zersetzung (psychological destabilization).

    Defenestration (roughly: leaving a building unwillingly by way of an upper floor window) seems
to have been invented at a 1419 incident in Prague, when a mob decided to toss some city officials who
refused to release the mob's associates from jail. Over the years it became an unofficial Czech method
of dealing with opponents and it reappeared in 1948 when foreign minister, Jan Masaryk, was thrown
from his bathroom window by the communists. His death was declared a suicide. It seems to have
returned to be a favorite method of dealing with "undesirables" in post-1990 Russia.

    Liquidation is the simple execution of enemies without the necessity of following legal procedure
(also called extrajudicial) and sometimes called assassination if the subject is of high political or military
stature. It is simple and ruthless. The killing of Nazi SS-General Reinhard Heydrich during WWII is
a good example, although he was deserving of his fate.[65]

---

[65] The assassination of Leon Trotsky, a central figure in the 1905 Russian Revolution, is one of the most well-known
liquidation examples. After the death of Lenin, he was a vocal critic of Josef Stalin and fell out of favor before being
expelled from the USSR. Because of his continued work against Stalin, he was sentenced to death in absentia, tracked
down to Mexico City, and liquidated by an agent of the NKVD, a forerunner of the KGB. We won't dwell on Caesar here.

Zersetzung is a cunning and heartless method of reducing a subject's will to resist or oppose, often even their will to live. It was a form of extreme hazing — so-called "psychic demolition" — used extensively by the MfS "Stasi" mostly on dissidents and opposition figures within East Germany. Covert methods of abusive control and psychological manipulation were used to disrupt the target's private or family life so as to disable their activities against the "communist paradise." to systematically intimidate individuals or groups, to ruin their reputations, isolate or criminalize them. Friendships were destroyed, and professional careers ruined without the victims even realizing why.[66]

As told by East German historian Hurburtus Knabe, "The goal was to destroy secretly the self-confidence of people, for example by damaging their reputation, by organizing failures in their work, and by destroying their personal relationships. In this matter, East Germany was a very modern dictatorship. The Stasi didn't try to arrest every dissident. It preferred to paralyze them, and it could do so because it had access to so much personal information and access to so many institutions."

Perhaps more eloquently, East German dissident Jürgen Fuchs wrote that Stasi's goal was "the disintegration of the soul."[67]

The Cases

Otto John

Mysterious to this day, is the defection or — as he himself insisted — the kidnapping of West German spy[68] Otto John by the *Stasi* to the East. It remains as one of the more bizarre episodes in the spy history of Berlin and the first "defection" of an BRD official to the East.

Prior to WWII, John was an opponent of Adolf Hitler and a member of the conspiracy to assassinate him on 20 July 1944. He escaped to England to avoid execution and returned to Germany after the war, where he assisted with the prosecution of Nazi officials at the Nürnberg Trials.

On 4 December 1950, he was appointed President of the West German Federal Office for the Protection of the Constitution *(Bundesamt für Verfassungsschutz)* with the support of the British government. Chancellor Konrad Adenauer, however, didn't trust him. His colleagues at the Gehlen Organization (OG), many of whom were former members of Germany's military intelligence during the war, also considered him a traitor for his contacts with the conspirators.[69]

Otto John was a vocal opponent of West Germany's rearmament and the employment of former Nazis in the government. That may have led him to what came next. On 19 July 1954, he flew to West Berlin for a memorial of the victims of the 20 July assassination attempt which was held at the Bendler Block. Following the event he met a friend, Wolfgang Wohlgemuth, a doctor from East Berlin with communist sympathies, near his Uhlandstraße 175 home (probably at the Schildkröte restaurant), who drove him across the border into the Soviet Zone of East Berlin. Shortly thereafter, the GDR press gleefully announced John's defection. A month later he met the press in East Berlin and declared, "After careful consideration, I decided to go to the GDR and stay here because I see the best opportunities here to work for the reunification of Germany and against the threat of a new war."

---

[66] MfS-Lexicon, BStU-Berlin, Bundesarchiv.
[67] Burkhard Bilger, "The Stasi Files," The New Yorker, June 3, 2024. (Vol C, No 15), New York: Conde Nast, 2024.
[68] John was a member of the resistance against Hitler and a participant in the 20.Juli Plot.
[69] The Gehlen Organization was supported by the Americans, while the British supported the BfV.

The restaurant "Schildkröte" near Wohlgemuth's office at Uhlandstraße 175

While John allegedly wanted to work for peace, the Soviets had other ideas. He went to Moscow where the Russians explained that he should make a definitive break with the Adenauer government and speak against West Germany's policies. It became clear to John that his plan was an illusion and he was a pawn in the middle of a game between two governments. He returned to East Berlin in December 1954. By this time, he was under continual surveillance and was only able to escape back to the West at the end of 1955.

The damage had been done. The former chief of the BfV was put on trial where he insisted that he had been drugged and taken across the border by his former friend Wohlgemuth and that he had only spoken out against the West German government to make sure that he was safe in East Germany. John was convicted of treason and sentenced to four years in prison. He was pardoned four years later but never exonerated.

In 1997, "discoveries in documents from the archives of the KGB," were said to have contradicted his representations of innocence."[70] Markus Wolf, in his biography *The Man Without A Face*, contradicted that story and said John had indeed been abducted by the East German government.

— Wohlgemuth's office at Uhlandstraße 175, U-Bahnhof Uhlandstraße (U2)

---

[70] *Suddeutsche Zeitung,* 29 March 1997.

Walter Linse — A man without hope

The man who left his apartment that morning knew he was a possible target. He'd told friends and colleagues that you shouldn't work against the communists unless you were prepared to pay a price.

Dr. Walter Linse was one of those people.

The Soviet Union had a long history of eliminating troublesome people whether they were members of the opposition, politicians who have fallen from favor, or military officers who had become suspect. Not only indigenous Russians but foreign nationals were often victims of Soviet executive action.

Former politicians and citizens of satellite countries who turned against the Soviet regime were also targets. In the latter case, actions against such individuals were usually carried out through the corresponding satellite intelligence service, aided and abetted by Soviet state security. The abduction of Dr. Walter Linse exemplifies this type of operation.

Born in Chemnitz, Germany in 1903, Linse was driven to excel and became a lawyer and beyond that received a Doctorate of Law. By 1938, he was employed with the Chemnitz Chamber of Commerce and Industry (IHK) as its "Aryanization Officer," (responsible for closing down Jewish businesses) so there can be no doubt that he was involved in Nazi injustice. He stayed in that role until the end of the war.

After the arrival of Soviet occupation forces, Linse did his best to disavow any role with the NSDAP claiming to be a member of an anti-nazi resistance group called "Ciphero," an organization that seems to have existed only in his mind. But slowly the walls closed in and Linse felt his history with the Nazi Party and the IHK would become public and end his career.

In June 1948 the time had come: Walter Linse and his wife fled to Berlin, the focal point of the East-West conflict. Berlin was also a playground for the international secret services and Walter Linse had jumped from the frying pan to the fire. He soon joined an organization concerned with human rights abuses in the East: the *Untersuchungsausschuss freiheitlicher Juristen* (UfJ) or "Society of Free Jurists." The UfJ was anti-communist.

The UfJ was founded in West Berlin in 1949. It provided lawyers and free legal advice to persons who had fled the Soviet Occupation Zone. Sometimes 200 people came each day. Often, the newly arrived provided information about events in the GDR that with the UfJ's analysis was of interest to intelligence agencies. As its reach into the East became more appreciated, the CIA began to provide financing in the 1950s and the UfJ was considered for a role in an eventual role in future conflict. The UfJ even helped form groups equipped with radios that were to operate behind the lines in the event of war. Such plans were soon abandoned, but the damage was done and the East Germans and Soviets considered it a particularly dangerous organization.

Stasi Deputy Erich Mielke was exceptionally concerned with the UfJ and created a special element within Section V (Pursuit of Internal Opposition) to deal with it. In 1951, *Stasi* succeeded in infiltrating an agent named Ruth Schramm, into the UfJ who began to report on the workings of the group and provided the name of East Berliners who visited it (remember this is before the Wall went up). Through Schramm's information, Walter Linse was identified and targeted for kidnapping. It became a personal crusade for Mielke but he was only able to undertake this with the consent of the "friends," i.e., the Soviet MGB.[71]

---

[71] The MGB was the predecessor of the KGB.

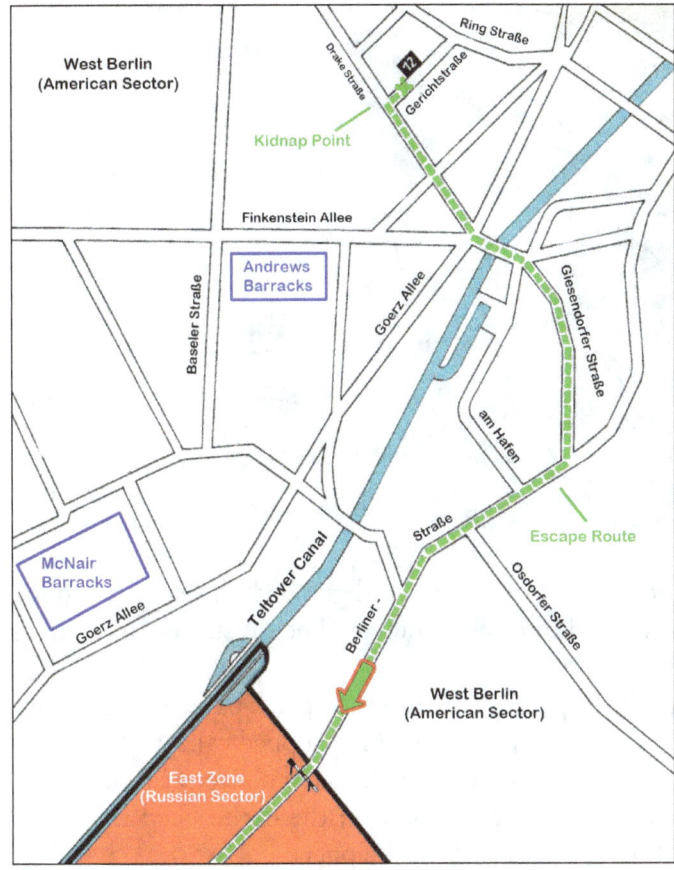

Map of Linse Kidnap / Escape Route (credit: BA - Lageplan 1952 Untersuchungsausschuss freiheitlicher Juristen B 209 /1200)

To conduct the "snatch" the MfS recruited criminals. Given overall responsibility MfS officer Paul Marustzök chose a gang of hardened baddies including Siegfried Benter, Herbert Krüger and Kurt Knobloch.

Marustzök "procured" (stole) an Opel Kapitan off the Kurfürstendamm and on the evening of July 2, 1952, the kidnappers gathered in Karlshorst, where Bennewitz took charge. With everyone briefed on how things would go down, they set off the next morning in the Opel to Linse's home in Lichterfelde at Gerichtsstraße 12 .

Normally, Linse left for work around 7:30 a.m. Bennewitz and Knobloch planned to grab him and put him in the car, but a dog-walking passerby disturbed them and they abandoned the attempt. They came back on July 8, 1952 this time better prepared. The Opel had been disguised as a Berlin taxi (painted black) with a stolen registration plate obtained from another West Berlin cab that had been stopped in the East.

Benter had been replaced by a professional wrestler Kurt Borchard. His job would be to subdue Linse. Marustzök also provided the criminals with four pistols.

As expected, Dr. Linse left the house on time. Once on the sidewalk, Borchard approached and asked Linse the time and a light for his cigarette. When Dr. Linse started to pull out matches, Borchard grabbed him and wrapped his other arm around Linse's neck. Linse, however, broke free and ran towards the taxi, which he mistakenly thought would help him.

Linse Home on the former Gerichtsstraße in direction of escape towards Drake Straße (credit: author)

Bennewitz was standing next to it and Kruger at the wheel. Borchard grabbed Linse again and fell into the back seat with the victim as Bennewitz jumped into the front seat. The car started forward as Knobloch was getting in and took off at high speed.

A woman who witnessed the event cried out for help and a the driver of truck parked nearby gave chase. The kidnappers in the car fired shots at the truck with a pistol and dropped caltrops[72] to deter the chase. The truck driver later testified that he had been shot at. He hailed a police car to tell them what had happened. The police chased the Opel but they were too late; the car reached the sector border where the guards were ready and opened the barrier for the kidnappers.

On the other side, Marustzök was waiting. He paid each kidnapper 1,000 West Marks and took them off to a safe-house where they were hidden for several days. Linse was taken directly to Hohenschönhausen Prison. With Erich Mielke's "arrest warrant," Linse was interrogated for up to 18 hours a day with Russian MGB officers always present. According to *Stasi* files discovered after 1990, Linse provided information of limited value. Internally, however, the Soviet MGB described the kidnapping as a great success.

On September 23, 1953, a Soviet military tribunal met in Karlshorst and sentenced Linse to the "maximum penalty" — death by firing squad — for espionage and anti-Soviet propaganda. Linse was transported to Lubyanka Prison in Moscow for his execution, where he was reportedly shot on December 15, 1953.

The kidnapping did not enhance East Germany's reputation in the West.

Linse's death was announced in a statement issued by the Soviet Red Cross in June 1960, a virtual admission of Soviet responsibility for the kidnapping. The cited date of his death is unconfirmed as information from fellow prisoners of Linse reported him alive as late as 1955.[73]

Gerichtsstraße, the street on which Linse's home was located, was named Walter-Linse-Straße.

Kidnap Site, Walter-Linse-Straße 12, Lichterfelde-Süd, S-Bahnhof Lichterfelde-Ost (S25/S26).

---

[72] Caltrops are devices made of sharp spikes dropped on a roadway to slow following vehicles.
[73] Klaus Bästlein, Vom *NS-Täter zum Opfer des Stalinismus;* John Prados, ed., "The Secret War for Germany: CIA's Covert Role in Cold War Berlin Explored through Recently Declassified Documents."

If he had made it this far... Home Free — Friedrichstraße Bahnhof (credit: author)

Rendered Harmless - Czeslaw Kukuczka

Czeslaw Kukuczka just wanted out. He was a Polish firefighter and a father of three, he had a plan to leave the East Bloc. In 1974, he showed up at the Polish embassy in East Berlin with a briefcase and said it contained a bomb. There was no bomb.

The Polish delegation contacted the authorities and it was the MfS *Stasi* that responded. They had been given orders to handle the case expeditiously, so they took him to the Friedrichstraße Bahnhof and stamped his passport with five visas to pass all the control points for an easy exit.

After all, Friedrichstraße was the last stop before entering free West Berlin and if you made it that far, all should be in order.

At least that's what Czeslaw thought. The Stasi officers had other ideas, as they had been given the order to render Kukuczka harmless. According to witnesses, as the Pole approached the last check point, a Stasi officer stepped out of a hiding place and shot Kukuczka with a pistol twice in the back, mortally wounding him; he died soon after. Kukuczka was cremated and his ashes were sent to his family without any explanation.[74]

The officer, Martin Naumann, was decorated for his "special services."

It would have remained an unsolved case but the Wall went down and the Stasi's records became a matter of public record. The Berlin Prosecutor's Office was able to make a case against Naumann when the shredded files were reassembled in 2016 with the aid of a high-powered scanner and special software. Shortly thereafter, the Polish government issued a warrant for Naumann's arrest.[75]

Naumann, now 80 years old, was located living in retirement near Leipzig and put on trial in March of 2024. He was sentenced to ten years in prison on 14 October 2024. The fact that Naumann fired the rounds from behind and without any threat from Kukuczka, weighed heavily on the guilty verdict. His actions were deemed to have been "treacherous" and "malicious."

Of the 140 deaths involved with attempted escapes from East Berlin, Naumann was the first to have been successfully charged and convicted of murder. Of the other shooters, only a small number have been put on trial and most of those have received the lesser charge of manslaughter.

---

[74] Stefan Appelius, "Tod im Tränenpalast," article on-line: https://zeitschrift-fsed.fu-berlin.de, zdf 39/2016.

[75] "Czeslaw Jan Kukuczka" article on-line: http://www.berliner-mauer-gedenkstaette.de/en/1974-322,894,2.html.

Maison de France and a Personal Vendetta

The bomb went off precisely at 11:20 in the morning of 25 August 1983 on the fourth floor of the Maison de France (French Cultural Center) in Berlin. One man was killed and 23 injured in the blast, which was initially claimed by the "Secret Army for the Liberation of Armenia" (ASALA). Coincidentally, two bombs also exploded that day in Beirut at the barracks of French and American peacekeepers in Lebanon, which diverted public attention from Berlin. While the bombs in Beirut were planned and carried out by the Iranian-backed Islamic Jihad, the bomb in Berlin was actually planned and later claimed by avowed professional revolutionary "Carlos the Jackal," whose real name was Ilich Ramírez Sánchez.

Born in Venezuela, Carlos joined the communist party at an early age and received training in guerrilla warfare first at Camp Matanzas in Cuba and then in "active measures" at Patrice Lumumba University in Moscow (he was expelled for poor academics). He then travelled to Beirut, joined the Popular Front for the Liberation of Palestine (PFLP), and began a career that was tied to radical terrorist causes around the world, (attacks by the PFLP and the Japanese Red Army), before he went even more rogue and formed his own terror network called Organization of the Armed Arab Struggle (OAAS). After Carlos' wife, Magdalena Kopp, a West German terrorist in her own right, was captured by the French in 1982, Carlos began a series of reprisal actions against her captors. The bombing of the Maison de France was one of these.

Importantly, the East German MfS assisted in the operation. Explosives were smuggled into East Berlin by Johannes Weinrich, the German founder of the Revolutionary Cells (RZ) who had become a close associate of Carlos, but the material was confiscated when he arrived at Schönefeld airport. A senior Stasi officer, Lieutenant Colonel Helmut Voigt, who led Section 8 of the MfS's *Hauptabteilung XXII "Terrorabwehr"* (Main Department 22 - Counterterrorism) confirmed that Weinrich had brought the explosives into Germany to conduct a terrorist attack against the French in West Berlin and authorized the bomb-making material be given back to the group with the collaboration of a diplomat, inside the Syrian Embassy in East Berlin.[76]

Weinrich transported the explosives from East to West Berlin via the Friedrichstraße train station and gave them to a Lebanese associate of Carlos, Mustafa El-Sibai. El-Sibai planted the 24-kilos of explosives inside a closet within the Maison de France. When it exploded a German national, Michael Haritz, was killed and 24 others were wounded and the building was severely damaged. It re-opened in 1985.

But there were consequences...

Carlos was finally captured by the French DGSE in a Khartoum, Sudan hospital while he was in the middle of a surgical procedure. Sedated by a cooperative doctor, the French spirited him out of the hospital and onto an airplane bound for Paris. Tried for his multiple crimes, he received three life-sentences. Weinrich was captured in Yemen and was found guilty in a German trial and given a life sentence.

---

[76] Although HA XXII was ostensibly charged with defending the GDR from terrorist attack, it worked closely with left- and right-wing extremists, along with Arab terrorist groups which conducted terror attacks against West Germany and NATO countries. Radical western groups were seen as allies in the fight against the "decadent West" and support included providing safe-haven, training, and material for their operations. "Carlos" and his comrades found shelter in East Berlin and served the MfS as a source of information about the global terrorist scene. From 1983 onwards, however, efforts were made to get rid of the increasingly unwelcome guests. That said, in 1988, the MfS had working relationships with 50 members of 19 terrorist organizations — among then ETA, IRA, PLO, and the RAF. — Tobias Wunschik, *Die Hauptabteilung XXII,* Berlin: BSTU, 1996.

The French Cultural Center aka *Maison de France* (credit: author)

Ilich Ramírez Sánchez aka "Carlos the Jackal" passport photo under the assumed name Carlos Andres Martinez Torres (credit: PD)

In 1990, when Helmut Voight heard that former Stasi officers were being arrested by the newly reunified German government, he escaped Germany.[77] He sought refuge in Volos, Greece but was arrested when his wife visited him in 1991, her baggage having been secretly tagged with tracking devices by West German investigators. A Syrian diplomat, Nabil Charitah, gave evidence against Voight at his trial. The judge declared that there was ample evidence to convict Voight and that the former East German government and the *Stasi* in particular, considered the terrorists to be "comrades in the struggle against imperialism and the class enemy" — meaning France and West Germany. For his role, Voight was found guilty and was sentenced to four years in prison.

The French Cultural Center boasts a library, bookstore, cafe, and a theater.

— Maison de France (Institut Français Berlin), Kurfürstendamm 21, U-Bahnhof Uhlandstraße (U1)

---

[77] Based on newly found information in the MfS *Stasi* archives.

MfS *Stasi* Surveillance Photo of La Belle Bombing Suspects outside the Libyan Embassy in East Berlin (credit: BStU MfS AIM Nr-25400-91-Tl-2/Bd-1/Bl-071/0824fb8464)

Exterior photo of former La Belle Disco and Memorial plaque (credit: author)

La Belle — a Berlin disco bombed

"A bomb has exploded in a crowded discotheque in Berlin, Germany, killing two and injuring at least 120, including more than 40 Americans. American authorities in Berlin said the two dead were an American soldier and a Turkish woman of 28. The bomb went off at 0150 local time (2350 GMT) when La Belle disco was packed with nearly 500 people." — BBC News, 5 April 1986

If you had been in the area that night, as I was, you would have heard the explosion. I was sleeping when it happened, but the "La Belle" wasn't far from my apartment and I heard the bomb go off. I got out of the bed and stood by the window trying to figure out what had happened. Then I heard the sirens, lots of them. I saw the *Feuerwehr* trucks go by and then some ambulances. That's when I knew it must have been bad. I went back to sleep. It was only when I got to work that I heard the story. We would go on alert for a possible mission soon, but it was countermanded soon after. The Reagan administration had come up with a different plan.

The "La Belle" bombing was the result of a series of tit-for-tat confrontations that started around 1981 in the Gulf of Sirte which Libya claimed as sovereign territory. Libyan leader Muammar Gaddafi and U.S. President Ronald Reagan already reviled each other primarily over Gaddafi's support for "liberation movements" worldwide. The U.S. saw it from a different perspective, it was more like direct support for international terrorism.

In 1981, the U.S. Sixth Fleet sailed into the Gulf of Sirte (recognized as international waters) as a freedom of navigation exercise. They returned several months later and shot down two Libyan aircraft that approached the fleet and refused to turn around when warned off. In 1985, Libyan support for the Palestinian Abu Nidal group led the U.S. to declare an embargo and several months later the Sixth Fleet returned to the Gulf of Sirte where it attacked Libyan patrol boats and onshore anti-aircraft missile sites that threatened the U.S. ships.

The "La Belle" bombing in Berlin was Libya's response.

The bomb was brought into the disco by a woman who left shortly before it went off. Two male soldiers and a civilian woman were killed and nearly 230 injured.

At first, terror groups like the German Red Army Faction were suspected, but U.S. intelligence intercepted and translated compromising messages from the Libyan Embassy in East Berlin. Those messages stated: "Expect the result tomorrow morning. It is God's will," (sent on the night of the attack) and then another that said: "at 1:30 am, one of the acts was carried out with success, without leaving no trace." A mission to capture the Libyan diplomats in East Berlin was briefly considered but rejected and a much more forceful decision was made.

All the time, the Stasi was fully aware of the situation. It had picked up information that three possible targets were considered for the attack: the "Nashville" discotheque on Breitenbachplatz, "Stardust" on Goerzallee, and "La Belle" on Hauptstrasse in Friedenau. An informant close to the Libyan Embassy even called his control officer the evening prior to let him know the attack was about to happen. In the end, the Stasi did nothing.[78]

The policy of the MfS was simple: do nothing that would harm the reputation of the GDR. Had they revealed the information, other countries would have questioned why they had not prevented the attack. It was better to remain silent. Further, they knew full well that diplomatic personnel were hardly checked at the border between East and West Berlin and certain embassies had indeed smuggled weapons and explosives across the Wall with impunity. The Stasi felt it was better to look away than to complicate diplomatic ties between the SED and friendly regimes, even if they were unfriendly to the West.[79]

Ultimately, the MfS acted with the principle that as long as terrorists did not attack the GDR, they were allowed to do as they pleased and the risk to the "opposition" was accepted. Essentially they were saying that the enemy of their enemy must be their friend.

Lacking specific information on which Libyan diplomats to capture, the U.S. launched bombing raids against Tripoli and Benghazi, including Colonel Gaddafi's residence in Tripoli. Libya answered with the December 1988 the bombing of a Pan-Am jumbo jet as it flew over the Scottish town of Lockerbie that killed 270 people.

As a postscript, when the United States specifically asked representatives of the GDR about the attack on "La Belle" in 1998, they denied the existence of any evidence of the Libyan embassy's involvement. (They also denied that "Carlos" had ever been in the GDR, which the U.S. knew to be untrue.)

It was only after Germany's so-called Peaceful Revolution that documents from the Stasi's archives gave up evidence that permitted the conviction of the perpetrators — Musbah Abdulghasem Eter, a Libyan diplomat and Stasi cooperative agent, Yasir Mohammed Shraydi, a Palestinian, the German woman who carried the bomb into the disco, Verena Chanaa, and her husband, Ali Chanaa, a Palestinian-German. All were sentenced to prison terms of between 12 and 14 years in 2001. In 2004, Libya agreed to pay a total of $35 million compensation to non-US citizens. In October 2008, Libya paid $1.5 billion into a fund to compensate relatives of the Lockerbie bombing, the American victims of the La Belle bombing as well as the 1989 UTA Flight 772 bombing, and the Libyan victims of the 1986 US bombing of Tripoli and Benghazi.[80]

— "La Belle," Hauptstraße 78, U-Bahnhof Friedrich-Wilhelm-Platz (U9).

---

[78] BStU, Thesenzuarbeit für Erich Mielke in Vorbereitung der Antiterrorismuskonsultationen der DDR mit den USA Signatur: BStU, MfS, HA XXII, Nr. 18138, Bd. 1, Bl. 158-171.

[79] In German, this is "Sankt-Florians-Prinzip" — the "Florian Principle" or roughly "O Holy St. Florian, please spare my house, set fire to another one".

[80] "Libya compensates terror victims," BBC News. 31 October 2008.

Mykonos — Assassins of the Ayatollah come to Town

17 September 1992.

It should have been a quiet night out. The Mykonos Greek restaurant was a gathering place for Berliners as well as émigrés who wanted to discuss politics in a secluded location. Unfortunately, the émigrés used the same place once too often. That evening, Democratic Party of Iranian Kurdistan (KDPI) opposition leaders Sadegh Sharafkandi, Fattah Abdoli, Homayoun Ardalan and their translator Nouri Dehkordi, were murdered as they sat in a small room in the back of the restaurant meeting with a number of other Iranian opposition members and guests.[81]

The Mykonos operation was authorized by the Iran's Special Affairs Committee, headed by Supreme Leader Ayatollah Ali Khamenei and included President Hojjatoleslam Akbar Hashemi Rafsanjani, Minister of Intelligence Hojjatoleslam Ali Fallahian and Foreign Minister Ali Akbar Velayati. The Committee gave the task to Hojjatoleslam Fallahian who assigned Special Operations Council officer Abdol-Rahman Banihashemi with conducting the operation. Banihashemi flew to Berlin and met with a local agent of the Ministry of Intelligence, Kazem Darabi, who worked as a grocer in Berlin. Once the plan was laid out, Darabi recruited four Lebanese Hezbollah operatives to assist in the operation, Youssef Mohamad el-Sayed Amin, Abbas Hossein Rhayel, Mohammad Atris, and Ataollah Ayad.

The assassination was a simple mafia-style execution. The killers knew of the meeting based on community messages and showed up just as it began. One man blocked the entrance, as Banihashemi entered the room shouting, "You sons of whores!" He began shooting, his fire directed at Sharafkandi, Ardalan, and Abdoli. After two bursts from Banihashemi's Uzi, Rhayel, an experienced Hezbollah operator, administered head shots to both Ardalan and Sharafkandi. Between them the assassins fired thirty shots in total.

Youssef Amin blocked the entrance to the restaurant. Farajollah Haidar drove the getaway car. Another Iranian known only as Mohammad had provided surveillance of the targets prior to the attack. Following the attack, Banihashemi, Haidar and Mohammad successfully escaped from Germany. The other Mykonos perpetrators were arrested. German prosecutors indicted Rhayel, Darabi and Amin each on four counts of murder and one count of attempted murder.

---

[81] The others present were Mehdi Ebrahimzadeh, Esfandiar Sadeghzadeh, Parviz Dastmalchi, Massoud Mirrashed, and Aziz Ghaffari, the owner.

Mykonos Memorial plaque. (credit: author)

Mykonos Exterior - now a German-Spanish Child-care Center (credit: author)

In its 10 April 1997 ruling, the German court issued an international arrest warrant for Iranian intelligence minister Ali Fallahian, declaring that the assassination had been ordered by him with the knowledge of Khamenei and Rafsanjani. Arrest warrants still stand for Abdol-Rahman Banihashemi and Haidar. All three are believed to be living in Iran

— Mykonos, Prager Straße 2a, The site now home to a child day-care center. U-Bahnhof Güntzelstraße (U9), Bus Stop Güntzelstraße (204)

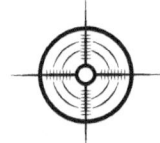

CHAPTER IX
Things Gone Bad

With the construction in 1961 of the intercity "anti-fascist protection barrier" aka "The Wall," East Germany effectively isolated West Berlin nearly completely from the East.

From August 13, 1961 forward, its primary purpose was achieved: to ensure East Germans could no longer flee to the capitalist West. But this also made it more difficult for the Western Powers to conduct intelligence operations in the East. To some extent, it also hampered the Soviet and East German activities but not to the same degree as for the Western services. To operate in the hermetically-sealed surveillance state of East Germany was much more difficult than the other way around.

For one, Russian KGB, GRU, and East German MfS officers could cross the border into West Berlin through special checkpoints separate from regular travelers. They had to show not only their identification but special permission orders signed by their supervisors that authorized the trip for operational purposes. While a KGB or MfS officer could defect, few did (Werner Stiller for one) as most East Bloc officers were ideologically reliable and the system that controlled their movement was difficult to circumvent even with their "privileges." That was not true in the opposite direction — western officers could easily cross the border and surrender themselves to the East Germans but few did. Mostly because they knew what lay on the other side.

That said, operations sometimes went sideways. With all the preparation, vetting, and verifying of assets, once in a while a bad choice was made either by the asset or the handler who thought he had things under control.

The Bullet that Changed Everything - Karl-Heinz Kurras, the *Stasi*, & the Death of a Student

West Berlin Police Officer Karl-Heinz Kurras' collaboration with the MfS began in 1955. Kurras reported to an office of the SED Party in East Berlin - and wanted to speak to the Stasi. After verifying that he was indeed a police officer, the Stasi officer asked him what he wanted. Kurras wanted to move to the East and join the *Volkspolizei*, but he would first have to prove his honesty. The best way would be to remain in the West and provide information about the West Berlin police. He agreed and returned to Charlottenburg where he quickly established himself as an informant inside the West Berlin *Polizei* and his handling officer was able to confirm his socialist leanings. Before long, he became *Geheime Mitarbeiter (GM)*, code-named "Otto Bohl."[82]

He was met by a number of couriers inside West Berlin, usually pensioners who could easily travel back and from between the Soviet and the Allied Zones. Older women made the ideal candidate for the job because no one considered the possibility that they would be working for an intelligence agency.

---

[82] GM - Secret Collaborator. A cooperative agent, recruited and paid, with access to an "enemy" organization.

Zoo Bahnhof — 1984 (credit: R. Schreiber) Zoo Bahnhof — 2024 (credit: author)

From a position in the operational command of the Berlin-Charlottenburg police district, he provided all the internal information he could on investigations, crime reports and personality profiles of other officers. Information that would help the Stasi and the GDR government should war ever come.

The collaboration was fruitful and worthwhile for both sides: the MfS obtained important information from within the West Berlin police. Kurras, received recognition, was paid regularly and even given access to firearms for his collection.[83] Kurras even secretly became a member of the SED.

Following the instructions of his 1st handling officer, *Stasi* Lieutenant Fritz Redlin, Kurras made a career in the police and then moved to the *Kriminalpolizei (Kripo)*, the criminal investigation department. In 1965, he transferred again to a department within *Kripo* that was responsible for protecting the police against infiltration attempts from East Germany. This sensitive area of the West Berlin police had been a top target for the MfS and now Kurras was inside.

On May 16, 1967, Kurras met GHI "Winter," his courier at the *Schleusenkrug* in Berlin's Tiergarten.[84] He had already given *Stasi* the security details on the upcoming visit of the Shah of Iran. This time he said the police would go to Readiness Level I because a number of assassination threats had been received.[85]

"Winter" noted in her meeting report that "Otto Bohl" currently seems overworked and has become more nervous. During the course of the conversation he also said that the work was really getting on his nerves." It was the last operational meeting "Otto Bohl" would have with his *Stasi* employers.

On 2 June 1967, Police Detective Karl-Heinz Kurras was on duty outside Deutsche Oper for the state visit of Shah Mohammad Reza Pahlavi, where a large student demonstration protesting the Shah's visit was taking place. During the event Kurras pulled out his pistol and fatally shot student Benno Ohnesorg in the back of the head. Later he claimed Ohnesorg had attacked him, a charge that was proven to be untrue. Kurras was acquitted, but at the time, most young Germans judged the proceedings to have been influenced by right-wing politicians.

The event was considered to be a political murder and became a beacon for the student movement while Kurras became the face of what they saw as the "fascist pig." The Socialist German Student Union (SDS) judged the Federal Republic of Germany to be fascist.

---

[83] Private ownership of pistols and other firearms was strictly controlled in West Berlin, even for police officers.
[84] GHI - Secret Main Informant. Only people who were absolutely reliable politically and trusted were considered for the position as a GHI. They sometimes handled other GM agents.
[85] BStU, Bericht über das Ergebnis eines Treffs zwischen GHI "Winter" und GM "Bohl," BStU, MfS, GH, Nr. 2/70, Bd. 2, Bl. 32-35.

The incident has been assessed as one of the key elements that led to the rise of terrorist movements in Germany such as the 2 June Movement and the Red Army Faction (RAF). Gudrun Ensslin, who would later become an RAF terrorist said that because of the incident, "We must arm ourselves."

Allegedly, the Stasi leadership went in a panic when it learned of the incident. Kurras's *Führungsoffizier* (handling officer) was horrified. "It is still difficult to understand how this GM could commit such an act, even if it was caused in the heat of the moment or through negligence, since it is a crime." The Stasi quickly decided to break off all connections with Kurras and he was directed to destroy any evidence of his collaboration with East Germany.[86]

Kurras returned to duty with the police until his retirement in 1987, never wavering from his claim that he had been attacked. He once stated: "Anyone who attacks me will be destroyed."[87] He died in 2014.

It was only in 2009 after the fall of the Wall that Kurras's double-dealing with the *Stasi* and his membership in the communist party became known.[88] The implications of that relationship and what drove Kurras to commit the crime can only be speculated. What is known is that Karl-Heinz Kurras was probably the most important *Stasi* spy in West Berlin. That he was a *Stasi* asset is clear, but the level of *Stasi* participation — if any — in Ohnesorg's murder remains murky.

Berlin, January 26, 1965

Report

Meeting with "XXXXX"

Meeting time: 6 p.m.

Meeting location: "Kurt" — Kurt Schumacherplatz, Restaurant Wienerwald

At 4:00 p.m. I went through the checkpoint at Friedrichstrasse station and took the S-Bahn to Großgörschenstrasse. The checkpoint went without incident. Then I took the bus to the Zoo, where I changed to another bus to Charlottenburg. I took another bus and went to Leopoldplatz. I took the subway to Tegel and then back to Kurt Schumacherplatz. On the way I bought oranges at the KaDeWe. I checked the routes and didn't notice anything suspicious.

I entered the restaurant at exactly 6 p.m. Bohl arrived five minutes later. When I greeted him I immediately asked: Have you checked yourself thoroughly? Bohl said that he had been on the road since 5 p.m. and had taken a taxi on the way. We only ate in the restaurant and talked about trivial things.

██

██

████████████████████

We walked through lifeless streets to Wedding and made sure we were adequately covered.

Personally, he has no concerns.

The meet gave him some security. He was very happy with it.

We did not arrange a new meeting.

Signed XXXXXXX

---

[86] BStU, "Auskunftsbericht" vom 8. Juni 1967 über Karl-Heinz Kurras alias GM "Otto Bohl," BStU, MfS, GH, Nr. 2/70, Bd. 17, Bl. 109-115.
[87] Iken, Katja, Marc von Lüpke, "Ein Schuss, viele Fragen," Der Spiegel, Hamburg: SPIEGEL-Verlag, 18.02.2015.
[88] BStU, MfS, GH, Nr. 2/70, Bl. 5-7.

Operation Lake Terrace

When a Case Officer / Handler picks the wrong person to try to recruit, his mistake generally goes one of three ways: the candidate ignores the approach, he embarrasses the CO by reporting him publicly, or calls in the pros and they play a little game called "burn the spy." Of the three, the last one is the most fun, although it can be tricky.

Operation Lake Terrace was one of the latter.[89]

My unusual role in this began late in 1985 with the call from a friend. I knew she worked in CI but that was about it. She asked straight up if my car was running. I wasn't upset about that because my car did have some issues. A 1974 BMW 1600ti sedan, it was small and quite sporty. It was also German, a requirement for the task at hand. No other information was forthcoming.

I picked her up that evening near an apartment block and drove to a secluded street where she proceeded to slap a set of civilian license plates over my occupation forces plates. Now my car was truly a Berliner.

Driving through the streets as night fell to the French sector, she laid out the job. We were on surveillance for a possible take-down of a GRU officer who was scheduled to meet an American soldier he was trying to recruit.

The soldier in question had come onto the GRU's radar apparently because of a telephone call intercept. We knew the Russians and East Germans monitored our telephone calls in West Berlin — not just diplomats but ordinary soldiers and citizens as well. Apparently, the soldier had some financial issues and was talking to his state-side bank about an overdue payment on his car. Within a short time, an English-speaking man contacted him with an offer for a lucrative but confidential business venture and suggested a meeting. The soldier had paid attention in his OPSEC class and was suspicious. He contacted the Army's counter-intelligence office and reported the contact.

The army quickly decided that the approach was real and knew they might have an opportunity to burn the GRU but they had to interview the soldier to see if he was willing to play the game. He was and the CI officers briefed him on how the "op" would go down. They cautioned him not to travel with his contact to East Berlin and not to give whomever showed up at the first meeting any intelligence. "Just play along but be careful," they said.

They assumed that the Soviet would "cold pitch" the soldier, offer money, and say he was a GRU officer. After all, that seemed to be the GRU's style. The Soviets always seemed to believe American soldiers were greedy.

The first meeting happened at a restaurant on the Kurfürstendamm. A man approached and asked his name and then told the soldier to follow him. Nearby, the GRU officer introduced himself and made an offer: secrets for money. The GRU officer wanted the soldier to travel to East Berlin but he refused. Then he said, "Get some good material and to meet him in a couple of weeks." With that, he left.

The game played out with the soldier passing marginally classified information but the Russian began to complain that he needed better. Then contact was broken and months went by without any word. The GRU man reappeared suddenly, pretending that nothing had happened. The soldier's CI handlers decided the GRU must have been under a lot of pressure to produce, because they were

---

[89] The full story is detailed in the book *Traitors Among Us* by COL Stuart A. Herrington.

Photo of Benches where one KGB officer was apprehended. (credit: author)

Entrance to Tegeler Seeterrassen. (credit: author)

still willing to trust the young American. When they met again, he told the soldier to meet him at a restaurant in two weeks time and to bring the real secrets.

It was great news except that the restaurant, the *Tegeler Seeterrassen* (Lake Terrace) was in Tegel district inside the French Sector. The Americans didn't like to work in the French Sector because it meant that they would have to coordinate with their French counterparts — some of whom they didn't trust. But, apparently, my friend said, they worked through that because here we were in the French Sector. The game was on.

Everyone assumed the Soviets would be cautious and probably deploy counter-surveillance assets hours before the nighttime meet. They would be looking for any signs of surveillance, American occupation force license plates on cars, too many men of military age, all the usual things that could mess up an operation. That's why we went as a couples. We had multiple cars on the street with German civilian plates and made sure their people were well hidden. A couple of German-American CI agents (including a former Berlin Special Forces vet) and his "wife" went into the restaurant to observe.[90]

In order to detain the GRU officer, they needed to catch the exchange and ensure the soldier received money. Real classified information was also in the package to ensure charges would stick if any of the Soviets caught just happened not to be carrying diplomatic identity cards.

The soldier showed up and sat at a table and waited. An hour later, the Soviet hadn't shown and the Americans began to think of abandoning the effort. We sat in the car looking for suspicious people while listening to the hand-held radio for news. (I asked my friend how I was supposed to ID a Russian as I doubted they'd be wearing Ushanka hats inside West Berlin.) Nothing. Not a mouse was stirring.

The soldier finally gave it up and left, but as he was approaching his car, the GRU man approached. It seems he had waited outside not wanting to expose himself. He passed an envelope to and took the package from the soldier in return. Luckily, two American CI agents had not left and saw the pass. They rushed in and grabbed the GRU officer, calling out an alert. We closed down the area with some Berlin police and started identifying anyone in the area. Three additional GRU officers, all carrying Soviet Embassy identification, were picked up, one of whom thought he could elude the dragnet by sitting on a bench and reading a newspaper just outside the restaurant. Apparently, he failed to realize that reading a newspaper by the light of a streetlight looked odd.

We didn't participate in any of the apprehensions, so we bailed out when the excitement was over. I dropped my friend off at the American headquarters in a parking lot at the rear of Clay Compound. We took off the plates and I walked her to the front door as she still had to file her portion of the report on the evening' events. As we approached, we saw the four GRU officers being frog-marched to the front gate where they were turned over to a representative of the USSR's Consulate in West Berlin. They had been "interrogated" and given an offer to defect, but no one accepted. They probably were summoned back to the motherland soon after.

In this round at least, it was USA 4; USSR ø.

— Tegeler Seeterrassen, U-Bahnhof Alt-Tegel (U6), S-Bahnhof Tegel (S25), Bus Stop "Am Tegeler Hafen" (124, 125, 133, 222)

---

[90] The SF vet — an old friend of mine — told me of his role years later. At the time we didn't know who was "on the street" from our side.

CHAPTER X
"We have ways to make men talk."[91]

Some sights in Berlin are rather depressing, morbid even. One of these belongs to the Nazi era (1933-1945) and I will only mention it here as I found that it was quite depressing. That location is **Plötzensee Prison** *(Strafgefängnis Plötzensee)*, which is one of the most notorious places in the history of the city. It dates from 1879 and served as a prison and place of execution. Until 1933, there were less than 40 executions, but when Hitler came to power, the number jumped dramatically to around 2,900 persons hanged or guillotined, mostly members of the resistance or anti-Hitler movement. It serves now as a memorial "To the Victims of Hitler's Dictatorship of the Years 1933–1945."

— Gedenkstätte Plötzensee, Hüttigpfad, Charlottenburg, U-Bahnhof Turmstraße (U9) to Bus 123 Gedenkstätte Plötzensee, S-Bahnhof Beusselstraße (S41, S42) to Bus 123 Gedenkstätte Plötzensee.

Two other macabre Cold War sites will complete our list of painful places in Berlin.

Hohenschönhausen Prison

Following the German surrender in 1945, the Soviet NKVD took over the Hohenschönhausen area of northeast Berlin to use as a detention point. Called Special Camp No. 3, it served as a prison and transfer point. Over 20,000 people passed through their way to other Soviet camps to the East. The camp was closed in October 1946 and transformed into a prison. The basement cafeteria was converted by prison labour to a prison cell block called the U-Boot (submarine).

The MfS took control of the complex in 1951 and added new prison buildings that included 200 cells and interrogation rooms. After the Berlin Wall was erected in 1961, the prison was used to hold anyone who tried to escape East Germany. Many dissidents and political prisoners were also held there. The prison was a key component of the SED's system of political oppression. Instances of torture and physical violence were reported, especially in the 1950s, but psychological intimidation *(Zersetzung)* was the main method of political repression and techniques including sleep deprivation, total isolation, and threats to friends and family. Over 40,000 political prisoners were incarcerated here, including nearly every famous opponent of the regime.

---

[91] *The Lives of a Bengal Lancer,* Henry Hathaway, Paramount Pictures, 1935.

Hohenschönhausen Guard Tower. (credit: BA, MfS, HA IX, Fo, Nr. 2560, Bild 49)

Hohenschönhausen Guard Tower — 2024. (credit: author)

Hohenschönhausen Restricted Area — 1982. (credit: BStU)

Hohenschönhausen was largely not known to the populace during the SED regime for the simple fact that it was located in an exclusion zone, a large restricted area surrounded by military facilities. Officially, it did not exist and it did not appear on maps.[92] When the Wall fell, the prison wasn't stormed and prison authorities were able to destroy the evidence of their activities. Former prisoners have given testimony to reconstruct much of the information along with documents from other East German agencies.

The site has featured in movie and television, including *The Lives of Others* and *The Same Sky*.

— Berlin-Hohenschönhausen Memorial, Genslerstraße 66, Bus Stop Große-Leege-Straße/ Freienwalder Straße (256, N56)

---

[92] Period West German maps show the area as an empty block.

Spandau Prison

During the night of May 10, 1941, a specially-equipped Messerschmidt Bf 110E-1/N fighter-bomber droned across the English Channel toward Scotland. Reaching landfall, the lone pilot opened the canopy and tumbled out, opened his parachute and landed south of Glasgow in a field where he was apprehended. The pilot was Rudolf Hess, formerly Adolf Hitler's number two man. Ostensibly, Hess was on a personal peace mission but the British thought he was a bit looney and stuck him in prison. Hitler put out a kill on sight order and washed his hands of Hess. When the war ended, Hess was sentenced to life in prison for war crimes and sent back to Germany to live out his sentence in Berlin's Spandau Prison. He was joined by a six of Hitler's other lieutenants who had escaped the death penalty. By the time Hess committed suicide in 1987 at the age of 92, all the other prisoners already had died or been released.

Spandau Prison was built in 1876 and initially served as a military prison with space for up to 600 inmates. In the early days of the Third Reich, it served as one of the first concentration camps until 1933 when purpose-built camps were constructed. At the end of WWII, Spandau was put into use by the Four Powers as a place to incarcerate former Nazi officials who were sentenced at the Nürnberg Trials. The prisoners were Politician Baldur von Schirach, Admiral Karl Dönitz, Diplomat Konstantin von Neurath, Admiral Erich Raeder, Armament Minister Albert Speer, Minister for Economic Affairs Walther Funk, and Deputy Führer Rudolf Hess.

The four powers took turns guarding the prison. Despite the tensions between the Western Allies and the Soviets, the guard duty at the Spandau Prison was never impacted. A new guard platoon, made up of 37 soldiers and one officer, rotated in monthly with a change of the guard ceremony in front of the prison. The duty remained somewhat contentious during the Cold War because it gave the Soviets access to West Berlin. Some suspected the Russians were using the access to conduct espionage missions inside the western sector.

The prison was demolished in August 1987 after Hess's death to prevent it from becoming a neo-Nazi shrine. Everything from the prison was disposed of in the North Sea, or buried at the former RAF Gatow airbase. Almost everything anyway — a set of keys resides in the regimental museum of the King's Own Scottish Borderers in the UK.

A British Army store was built on the site, which was converted to a "Kaufland" convenience store after the Wall fell. Nothing exists on the site to tell anything of the former prison or its occupants.

— Spandau Prison site (now "Kaufland"), Wilhelmstraße 21-25.

Aerial View of Spandau Prison circa 1975. (credit: British Forces Berlin)

Surveillance Photo of Spandau with Russian Guard. (credit: author)

Where a Prison once stood, a "Kaufland" Parking Lot. (credit: author)

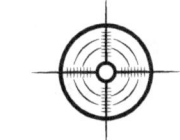

CHAPTER XI
Spy Meets and Spy Eats

Intelligence officers who want to recruit spies usually need to meet their target first. Diplomatic events provide one venue, but what if you're not under diplomatic cover or your potential recruitment isn't a diplomat? Office calls or "bumps" in public might work to get the ball rolling, but a quiet restaurant or bar is always good for further discussions that might lead to a recruitment. Once recruited, these spots might also serve as the location to have an extended conversation, that is, as long as you're not being watched. Berlin has many suitable locations and some of them already have their own secret history.

Ganymed

"Werner turned his head; the bushy black hair and dark skin made his white teeth flash like a toothpaste commercial. 'London wouldn't send you over here for that kind of circus, Bernie. For that kind of task they send office boys, people like me.'

'We'll go and get something to eat and drink, Werner,' I said. "Do you know some quiet restaurant where they have sausage and potatoes and good German beer?'

'I know just the place, Bernie. Straight up Friedrichstrasse, under the railway bridge at the S-Bahn station and it's on the left. On the bank of the Spree: Weinrestaurant Ganymed.'

'Very funny,' I said. Between us and the Ganymed there was a wall, machine guns, barbed wire, and two battalions of gun-toting bureaucrats. 'Turn this jalopy around and let's get out of here.' " - *Berlin Game,* Len Deighton

The Ganymed Weinrestaurant first opened its doors in 1931 and attracted all the "important" people of the capital city scene. A favorite of government boffins, diplomats in the Mitte district, it survived World War II and, during GDR times, cultural figures such as Bertolt Brecht and Helene Weigel often stopped by as it is next door to the Theater am Schiffbauerdamm, which hosted their plays. The chance to mingle with such luminaries, along with the excellent cuisine, brought in all sorts of interesting people who might fall prey to *Stasi* intelligence officers looking for possible targets to assess and recruit, especially legal travellers who came from the West to experience the culture. It was a good spot to find someone susceptible to a few extra D-Marks or watch someone fall prey to a honey trap set up in the bar. Even today, being close to the theater home of the Berliner Ensemble it is a good before or after event meeting point. The restaurant is still there, slightly transformed into a "brasserie" but it ranks as one of the best restaurants in Berlin with a spectacular location very near to the Frederick Straße Bahnhof on the East bank of the Spree River.

— Ganymed, Schiffbauerdamm 5, Friedrichstraße Bahnhof (S1 S2, S3, S5, S7, S9, S25, RE21, RE29), Tram (M1, 12)

Ganymed Grill Brasserie
(credit: author)

Ganymed from the
Friedrichstraße Bahnhof
across Spree River
(credit: author)

Schleusenkrug Beer Garden. (credit: author)

The side exit for fast get aways… (credit: author)

Schnitzel Beer Garden Style (credit: author)

Schleusenkrug

According to internal Stasi files, the Schleusenkrug was often used for agent meets.[93] Karl-Heinz Kurras, a West Berlin police officer who offered his services to the Stasi in 1955, met his handler here often to talk about operational as well as personal issues (at certain moments, his handler described an agent under great stress).

MfS operational notes describe a site that is close to several transport hubs, has many walking paths, the Berliner Zoo, and the Ku'damm. Close to secluded paths around the Berlin Zoo, isolated streets, and a busy train station, it's easily accessible and an ideal place to disappear into (and out of) for a quick personal meeting or an extended briefing.

If you're walking this area today, it's also a good place to stop and take a break from the chaotic Kurfürstendamm and city center. A refreshing drink or a Schnitzel and beer is good on a nice spring, summer, or fall day.

— Schleusenkrug, Müller-Breslau-Straße 14b, U-Bahn & S-Bahnhof-Zoologischer Garten, S – Bahnhof-Tiergarten

---

[93] The word *Schleusen* can mean smuggle or, in this case, the locks of the nearby Landwehrkanal.

Prater Garten — Berlin's oldest Beer Garden

"**When the Prater Biergarten came into view, he thought of his return to Berlin in 1946… Fischer sat down at a small table and allowed himself the pleasure of a large Pils. When the rather buxom waitress returned with his drink he ordered one of the famous Prater Wiener Schnitzel and sat back to enjoy the scenery. The waitress was talkative and friendly, obviously having no idea she was talking with a senior Stasi officer. Of course, Fischer made no mention of it; he didn't allow his position to intrude into his personal life.**" — *A Question of Time,* James Stejskal.

Serving patrons since 1837, the Prater Garten is fully intertwined with the cultural fabric of Berlin. It lies in Prenzlauer Berg, one of the quirkiest and socially adaptable districts of the city.

Since its beginning, it has been a focal point for theatre, political discourse, and other public gatherings. The Prater escaped the war more or less untouched and, before long, it was again the cultural hub of what would become East Berlin. It has featured theatre and musical performances, political gatherings for discussion and debate, along with films and variety shows.

Almost all of the restaurants in the East were controlled by the *Handelsorganisation*, the state trade organization that ensured both mediocre food and service at its unfortunate worst. The Prater was independent of the *HO* and its proprietors and workers actually cared about customers and the service it provided, factors that ensured its survival.

During the communist era, the government used the Prater to promote communism and German-Soviet friendship. There were obligatory festivals often followed by more interesting stage performances. In time, it became a cultural icon that subtly encouraged an alternative lifestyle inside a communist state. Maxim Gorki's plays that depicted Soviet life at the most basic level were staged here. Ironically, Gorki's work, and others like it, were the threads that would slowly unravel the socialist dream. As the owners are proud to say, it is part of the essence of Berlin.

— Pratergarten, Kastanienallee 7-9, Prenzlauer Berg, U-Bahnhof Eberswalder Straße (U2). Tram (M1, M10, M12), Bus (N2, N42)

Prater Garten, May 1st 1960, "Volksfest," (credit: BA Bild 183-72750-0057/CC-BY-SA 3.0)

Prater Garden — 2024 (credit: author)

Seeterrassen Menu
(credit: author)

Tegeler Seeterrassen

"Fish, favorite dish," a *Berlinerin* said to me one time. If that's true for you, the Seeterrassen is your place, especially on a nice day when you can sit and enjoy the scenery of Tegel Lake (Tegeler See). The menu is, for the most part, an offering typical fresh-water catch, although the airport is nearby and ocean creatures often make it to the table. I can handle almost everything except for the *Aal in grüner Soße* or Eel in Green Sauce.

Few people who walk by the restaurant or even those who eat there know of its secret history, but it served as the highpoint for Operation Lake Terrace, an American takedown of several Soviet GRU intelligence officers who were attempting to recruit an American soldier.[94]

Tegeler Seeterrassen, U-Bahnhof Alt-Tegel (U6), S-Bahnhof Tegel (S25), Bus Stop "Am Tegeler Hafen" (124, 125, 133, 222)

---

[94] OP Lake Terrace is described in Chapter iX — By the way, no one said the codenames were clever or original.

PM "Doner" at Hasir (credit: author)

The knife man at Hasir (credit: author)

The famous Hasir Doner (credit: author)

Hasir Ocakbası

Where else would the "Meister" meet his *Stasi IM* contact? In this "ethnic" Turkish restaurant, close to public transport and in Neuköln, a neighborhood where strangers stand out.

Hasir claims to be the restaurant which created the first Döner Kebab. This assertion is disputed by another Turkish Berliner Kadir Nurman, a food stand owner who had a *Buden* near the Bahnhof. But both those contentions are scoffed at by Turkish chefs back in the homeland who simply say *"Zirva."*[95]

What is true is that the Berlin variant is what we're all used to in the West. Picture an ice-cream cone shaped stack of meat (beef and/or lamb) cooking on a vertical spit. A generous portion is shaved off, stuffed in a pita with pickles, onions, tomato, and a garlic yoghurt sauce. Whatever you call it, Döner, Shawarma, or Gyro, it's the perfect thing to eat on the run. I should note that there are variants intended to cater to the tastes of others, which use chicken and even a vegetarian version exists — although I'm uncertain why.

Food can be ordered from the street window, which makes it a good cover stop as you can stand on the sidewalk and watch everyone while waiting for your order. Or a table can be had on the inside for a quiet meeting — that is, if the coast is clear.

In case you want to try another Döner spot, there are roughly 1300 Döner Buden (stalls) in Berlin.

Hasir is located at Adalbertstraße 12, U-Bahnhof Kottbusser Tor (U1)

---

[95] "Bull."

Rotes Rathaus

Built in 1861, damaged heavily in WWII, the reconstructed Rotes Rathaus served as the town hall of East Berlin from 1948 to 1991. *The Rotes Rathaus* or Red City Hall, figuratively designated the socialist government of East Berlin. It is now home to the mayor of Berlin and its government, the Berlin Senate. During the Cold War, the basement housed a restaurant called the Ratskeller or Town Hall Cellar. Suitably medieval-ish, the restaurant offered government officials, tourists, and diplomats a good meal and the possibility of being approached by the lurking *Stasi* officers who perched there looking for easy targets.

All that remains of that restaurant today is a government *kantine*, which offers a sad version of the original menu. That said, the building's exterior and halls were used in the filming of the television series "Babylon Berlin" and are well worth visiting.

— Rotes Rathaus, Rathausstraße 14 near Alexanderplatz, Mitte.

The Ratskeller Menu — 1978
(author's collection)

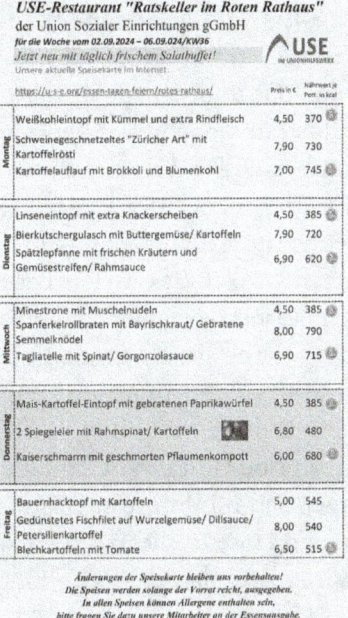

The Ratskeller Menu — 2024
(author's collection)

The Red Rathaus (credit: author)

KaDeWe — Kaufhaus des Westens

"Rabbit had one more trick to play. He walked north, stair-stepping through the neighborhood until he reached Kleiststraße, and then headed east toward KaDeWe, the largest department store in Germany. KaDeWe was the capital of capitalism on the continent, rivaled only by Harrods in London. With sixty thousand square meters of store and more than fifteen entrances, it was the mother of all surveillance nightmares. But the team didn't know that yet."

"Rabbit led them in a circle through the wild game section, followed by the fish, the cheese, then the bread section before he finally stopped at the center bar and ordered himself an Urquell. It was the "EndEx" signal and time for all to come together.
— *Appointment in Tehran,* James Stejskal

KaDeWe is one of the most famous landmarks in West Berlin and one of the largest department stores not only in Germany but Europe. Rebuilt after World War II, it was always a symbol of capitalism, and drew communist scorn. That said, the East German government tried to copy it with a socialist version in East Berlin called the *"Zentrum."* It was a poor attempt at mimicry, although the *Zentrum* was a great place to buy model railroad trains at a good price.

The 6th floor food hall of KaDeWe is a dietician's nightmare and continually expands year by year: it boasts 33 food stands with over 1000 seats. There are champagne bars, Veuve Cliquot and Moet, an oyster bar, sushi rolled by a sushi-master. It offers 1,200 kinds of sausages, 300 kinds of whiskey, 60 types of French bread, 1,300 varieties of cheese, not to mention paté, champagne, fresh fish and seafood, and, of course: *"Wild"* — fresh game like boar, pheasant, or venison.

Many espionage services recognized the building as an excellent place to conduct operations. With six huge floors to get lost on and multiple entry and exit points, it was easy to lose a surveillance team to conduct a quick meeting, or pass a package of information to an asset or a handling officer. In fact, on one occasion a team of American specialists who were conducting training inside the store, witnessed just such a "pass" and was able to alert German authorities to the participants' presence. Detained for "shop-lifting" the perpetrator turned out to be a drug dealer passing illicit substances. In any event, it was a moment to simultaneously illustrate possibilities and poor tradecraft.

In the 1980s, the East German *Stasi* conducted extensive casing of the store, one of the most famous landmarks in West Berlin. *Stasi* records exposed to the public after reunification showed it was interested in the store for its possibilities as a contact or meeting site. Photographs and written reporting documented the exterior and interior of the building including floor plans, as well as entrances from the street to the restaurant. The arrival and departure options by public transport, foot, and private vehicle are also recorded.

The reports resulted from the physical casing of the site by trained observers. Some reports were created as part of exercises and training for full-time and unofficial employees, while others were used to prepare for agent meetings. The *Stasi* checked the suitability of these sites to be used for such conspiratorial meetings beforehand. KaDeWe's 5th floor restaurant "Silberterrasse" was also examined as a potential meeting place for the *Stasi* with agents and informers. Personally, the *Pilsner Urquell* bar was my favorite meeting spot — small, hidden, and close to the exit points.

— KaDeWe, Tauentzienstrasse 21-24, Wittenbergplatz U-Bahnhof (U2, U3, U7), Bus Stop Wittenbergplatz (M46)

KaDeWe *Stasi* Surveillance
Photo (credit: BA, MfS,
HA VIII, Nr. 306, Bl. 44)

KaDeWe — 2024
(credit: author)

Kastanien Eck / Flying Monkey Bar - Oderberger / Kastanienallee

"A block later the sight of a tiny Kneipe, a corner pub, came into view ahead of him. He checked the street signs, Oderberger and Kastanienallee, and knew exactly where he was—the Prenzlauer Berg district—still a ways from the intercity border and safety.

What the hell, he decided and, needing a drink, stepped inside.

The Berliner Biere sign with a logo of a bear holding 3 beers above its head on either side of the entrance signaled what was on tap, not that there was much choice. The words "VEB Getränkekombinat" across the bottom reminded him he was still in a place where there were people's collectives for everything from farms to beer breweries to pubs… He'd sit for 30 minutes or so to see if any strange people came looking for him before starting out again."— *The Ratcatcher of Berlin,* James Stejskal

A neighborhood *lokale*, this place has been around quite a while, sitting on the corner of what was a gray neighborhood in East Berlin. It was a working class bar, but was sometimes used as a convenient stop to pass messages between friends (through a friendly barkeep) who couldn't otherwise see or telephone each other.

This popular bar was abandoned when the Wall fell, then a became restaurant. Prenzlauer Berg, a section of town that went from colorless during the Cold War, to rainbow with the coming of the new Berlin Counterculture. The area has been gentrified now, the price paid for its popularity, and to go with the new "Zeitgeist," the Flying Monkey offers contemporary "Chinese-inspired" cuisine.

— The Flying Monkey, Kastanienallee 15 at Oderberger, U-Bahnhof Eberswalder Straße (U2). Tram (M1, M10, M12), Bus (N2, N42)

Kastanien-Eck-Kneipe 1985 (credit: IMAGO/Christian Thiel)

Kastanien-Eck Flying Monkey 2024 (credit: author)

Savoy Times Bar
(credit: The Savoy)

The Savoy

"There were always bars to be found open on the Ku'damm, but Charlie had a specific one in mind and, when they ended up at the Savoy Hotel on Fasanenstraße, he declared it as if he was unveiling Tutankhamun's treasure.

"Here we are. The 'Times Bar' and they have great booze and good Cuban cigars."

"At this time of night?"

"This is Berlin. Where you been anyway?"— *The Ratcatcher of Berlin,* James Stejskal

Nobel Prize winner Thomas Mann once said of the Savoy, "We went to our familiar Hotel Savoy on Fasanenstraße... so pleasant and comfortable…"

The Savoy has stood in its city center location since 1929. On a quiet side street across from the historic Delphi Filmpalast and close to the Theater des Westens, other writers and artists besides Mann found their way here, among them, Henry Miller, Greta Garbo, and Maria Callas. And with good reason, the Times Bar is one of the best in the city with its own Cuban-licensed cigar shop, Casa del Habano, and — if you need some sleep — the rooms are great too.

The Savoy survived WWII unscathed and in 1945-1946, it served as the Headquarters of British Forces in Berlin before it was refurbished as one of the first hotels to reopen in the city.

The Savoy has not featured in any spy film because it stayed under the radar, one of the best kept secrets in the city. Where else could you bring a prospective recruit that offered a small, intimate setting, a dark corner to disappear into while cigars were smoked and the finest Scotch drunk as the case officer gave his perfect pitch. When a recruitment of a top flight source is in the wind, no expense is spared. And you don't give that secret up easily.

— Savoy Berlin, Fasanenstrasse 9-10, (currently being renovated), S+U-Bahnof Zoologischer Garten S3, S5, S7, S9, Bus Stop Theater des Westins 109, 110, M19, M29, M49, X34.

Imbiss Currywurst Stand at Wittenburgplatz (credit: author)

U.S. Special Forces (undercover) meet Bockwurst circa 1961 (credit: Jim Wilde)

Imbiss & Currywurst

We will end this section with an ode to Berlin's popular *Imbiss* stands. The word itself comes from Old German for "to bite" and has come to mean "snack." You will see them especially in the big cities like Berlin generally located in some stalls or street carts. They sell everything from *Knackewurst* and *Boülette* (a treat from the French Protestant Huguenot diaspora that settled in Berlin around 1700) to Berlin's most iconic food, the *Currywurst*. And don't forget the relative newcomer, the Döner Kebab, which arrived from Turkey circa 1970ish.

In 1949, Berlin was devastated by war and old man winter. No one had money and the food supply is dismal. A *Berlinerin by the name* of Herta Heuwer opened her *Imbiss* in Charlottenburg but struggled to find something that would sell and earn her some money. Not satisfied with a simple sausage and bread, she boils a bratwurst and then fries it, pouring on her special concoction of tomato ketchup, onions, and a heap of curry powder, which she has obtained from the British troops in the city. Normally, it's served with a big scoop of *Pommes* (fries) in a paper dish. In 1959, she even won a patent for this special sauce and at the height of her success, she was selling 10,000 a week.

Although Berliners in recent years have begun to warm to "foreign" foods like the Doner Kebab, they remain tenaciously loyal to their favorites like the humble Currywurst und Frites. Today in Berlin, more than 70 million of the ubiquitous currywurst are sold each year. They have been political and commercial fights over the origins and ownership of the sausage, with the city of Hamburg claiming the invention. Berliners usually just say *"Daß ist mir Wurst!"*[96]

For spies, an *Imbiss* can play an important role in setting up a surveillance detection route. Stopping at one gives the spy or handler a good opportunity to survey the area and see who might bear further watching. It's also a good place for a colleague to watch the officer's back to detect opposition tracking teams.

---

[96] I don't care!

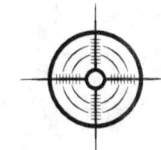

CHAPTER XII
One Final Win For The Good Guys & other tidbits from the Far Side...

Rosewood

"We blitzed Stasi Headquarters...We knew where we going. Had the map in our front pocket for decades. Their garden of earthly delights ignored, we hustled to the vault room. Detonated thermite charges to burn through locks and hinges, and left the bolts smoking so there'd be no doubt it was me."

Like the Pink Panther's glove," I said.

"Thanks, Clouseau." Muir went on. "East Germany's Crown Jewels disappeared from the most secure room in the most secure East German building forty-four minutes and forty-two seconds after the Wall came down."— *Muir's Gambit: A Spy Game Novel,* *Michael Frost Beckner*

The story of the "Rosewood" files (*Rosenholtz* in the Agency's misspelled version of the proper German word *Rosenholz*) remains one of the most tantalizing secrets of the CIA's Cold War successes. In 1989, when the Wall came down, the Stasi immediately began to destroy its files, but not all of them. The Crown Jewels were the files of Stasi's foreign intelligence department, the HVA — *Hauptverwaltung Aufklarung*. Those files listed all the agents Stasi had recruited outside East Germany, including all their spies inside the West German government and military, NATO, and other targets in Europe. In 1980, they suddenly appeared in the possession of the CIA at Langley.

How those files were obtained — whether the agency conducted a black bag job inside Building 15 (the HVA offices) at the MfS Normannenstraße or simply purchased them from a newly minted East German capitalist — remains somewhat of a mystery. Unless you were there.

Stasi Haus 15 & Haus 22 in foreground (credit: author)

Rosenholtz CD image (credit: author)

None more paranoid...

"Max Fischer began to close up his office. There was nothing he needed or wanted except for his personal Petschaft that he had used for his entire career. He slipped it back into his pocket after he pressed it into the bit of gray clay on his safe. And then he set a telltale as always, just in case. All secure."— *A Question of Time*

Stasi officers carried a seal called a *Petschaft*. A simple aluminum circle with a personal number and the words *Ministerium für Staatssicherheit* in a circle. The letter"A" indicated the Headquarters at Normannenstraße, while a "B" meant the holder belonged to any of the other offices across East Germany. It served as the final check on a locked door or safe when the officer checked out to go home after work or would be away for awhile. If the door was opened, the seal would show a crack. The seals couldn't easily be copied.

MfS *Stasi* "Petschaft"
Seal (credit: author)

Der Rote Koffer

Every poker player needs an ace up their sleeve. Erich Mielke kept his "ace" in *Der Rote Koffer,* a red suitcase locked in the safe in his office. His ace consisted of *"Kompromat"* — information with which he could blackmail SED Party Chairman Erich Honecker, including how Honecker confessed to Nazi interrogators and provided information that led to the exposure of a Czech spy and ultimately his entire anti-Hitler resistance group. The files also show that Honecker had given extensive testimony and thereby incriminated his fellow prisoners while he was in prison. That information contradicted the public image of Honecker as an exemplary communist resistance fighter.

Mielke's files also contained two petitions for clemency that Honecker's father had submitted to the Nazis for his son. The father stated that Honecker had renounced communism and was also prepared to fight for the Nazi state. Clearly, not things that would go over well with Honecker's supporters or his enemies.

Also in the suitcase were private letters from Honecker's wives to SED Chairman Walter Ulbricht, which each denounced the other to Ulbricht and a Stasi report on the renovation costs, paid with State funding, of a private bungalow that belonged to one of Honecker's lovers. The documents were Mielke's back-up plan for possible blackmail, but it was a plan he never put into play.

The Red Suitcase makes several appearances in the German TV espionage series, *Kleo,* as do interior shots of MfS Headquarters in Normannenstraße.

Red Suitcase (credit: author)

General Mielke in Gala Uniform (credit: PD)

General Mielke salutes Chairman Honeker in front of Stasi Headquarters (credit: BA, MfS, ZAIG, Fo, Nr. 885, Bild 157)

CHAPTER XIII
Books, Movies, and Faction[97]

In fiction, whether a novel or film, Berlin has always played a special role, a Cold War locale brimming in mystery, nuance, atmosphere.

Death on the Wall

"…Leamus pulled himself upward until he had reached the top of the wall. He tugged sharply at the lower strand of wire and it came toward him, already cut.

'Come on,' he whispered urgently, 'start climbing.'

Laying himself flat he reached down, grasped her up-stretched hand and began drawing her slowly upward.

Suddenly the whole world seemed to break into flame; from everywhere, from above and beside them, massive lights converged, bursting upon them with savage accuracy."
— *The Spy Who Came In From The Cold, John le Carré*

---

[97] Faction - a mix of fact and fiction in writing. Or, as Albert Camus put it: "Fiction is the lie through which we tell the truth."

Fiction or not, John le Carré described the world of espionage and treason with a deadly accuracy that was also infused with a sense of futility. He wasn't the first former intelligence officer to write novels, but he was one of the first to express his cynicism on the value of intelligence operations.

In *The Spy Who Came In From The Cold,* the author described the seeming duplicity and amorality of both the Soviet and British intelligence services. The scene above is the culmination of his tale. What le Carré did not describe were the many other deaths that took place because of the Wall and the determination of many East German citizens to escape their own country's repressive regime.

Alec Leamus and Liz Gold trying to climb over the Wall (credit: AI)

Checkpoint Charlie

"Don't forget, 007. You're on your own now."

With those words, British Secret Service Chief "M," bid farewell to the most famous secret agent in film history. Robert Brown played "M" while James Bond was played by Roger Moore in the film *Octopussy*. Filming began in Berlin and a number of promotional shots of Roger Moore as 007 were taken at prominent locations close to the Wall in August 1982.

One set location was at Checkpoint Charlie near the Military Police building on Friedrichstraße. As usual, the Stasi documented the preparations for the filming and recorded its observations in a report which was later recovered from the MfS Headquarters at Normannenstraße. While the Stasi observers didn't get a photo of Moore, they did capture British actor Robert Brown, in the role of "M," climbing out of the Mercedes Benz as Bond heads off to his assignment.

Unclear is whether the MfS screened the "007" film in their headquarters later. Germans weren't much into popcorn back then. Among the films shot at CP "Charlie" (or a facsimile thereof) were: *The Spy Who Came In From The Cold, Funeral in Berlin, Octopussy, Bridge of Spies,* and *The Man From U.N.C.L.E.*

— Checkpoint Charlie, Friedrichstraße and Kochstraße, U-Bahnhof Kochstraße (U6), Bus stop U-Bahn Kochstraße/Checkpoint Charlie (M29, N6)

"M" Robert Brown climbs out of BMW during filming at Checkpoint Charlie. (Quelle: BArch, MfS, HAVI, Nr. 182, Bl. 102 [Crop])

007 Octopussy — silhouette of 007 on Wall at Potsdamer Platz (credit: author & Photoshop)

The Assassin and the Hotel Brecker

It's nighttime and Jason Bourne, the Treadstone assassin Bourne, stands against the wall of the bathroom, dripping wet from the rain outside. He is looking at the reflection of a man in the mirror. It's his target, Neski, who just arrived and he's talking on the phone. Bourne prepares a syringe then hears the front door to Room 645 open once more.

It's Sonya Neski, his wife. The couple hugs.

Change in plan, Bourne pockets the syringe, and pulls out another weapon, a pistol. He checks the mirror and his pistol, then notices the mirror again.

The wife is coming into the bathroom. She sees him, frightened, she can't speak.

Bourne confronts her, finger up. "Shhh," he whispers.

As she backs out of the bathroom, Mr. Neski suddenly sees her and Bourne with the pistol.

Bourne doesn't hesitate — SNAP! One silenced shot. Neski goes down.

Bourne turns to a stunned Mrs. Neski, forces the gun into her hand, and shoots her in the heart." — *The Bourne Supremacy*, Robert Ludlum

Hotel Brecker doesn't exist in real life. The scene in *The Bourne Supremacy* was filmed at the real-life Cumberland Haus which is located at Kurfurstendamm 193. There are several good cover stops — cafés and shops — nearby.

— Cumberland Haus, Kurfurstendamm 193, U-Bahhof Uhlandstraße (U1), S-Bahn Savignyplatz (S3, S5, S7, S9), Bus M19, M29, X10, 109, 110, N10

Bourne's Hotel Becker is actually the Haus Cumberland, Kurfürstendamm 194 (credit: author)

Rote Burg 1908
(credit: PD)

Alexanderplatz, World Time Clock & the Pope's Revenge

In *The Bourne Supremacy,* man-on-a-mission Jason Bourne meets agent Nicky Parsons at the World Time Clock in the middle of Alexander Platz and then disappears into the crowd with the help of a street tram and an on-going street demonstration.

A special entry is needed for Babylon Berlin, the German television series, because so much of the city was used in its filming. The surrounding Alexander Platz was used extensively in the TV series, *Babylon Berlin*, albeit without the newer buildings like the TV tower or the World Time Clock.

The nearby *Rote Burg* (Red Castle) police headquarters was destroyed in WWII, but recreated with computer simulations. The *Rotes Rathaus* (Berlin City Hall) was used for closeup scenes involving the exterior of the police headquarters, because their red brick appearance and architectural style are very similar. Interiors of the police headquarters lobby were filmed at the *Rathaus Schöneberg*. A lengthy sequence was filmed at the historic *Theater am Schiffbauerdamm*, where the play ran at the time. The Ganymed Weinrestaurant is nearby.

The Red Castle, home to Berlin's main police station, depicted in the movie is no more. Now a pink-hued department store, "Alexa," sits on its former site at Gruenerstraße and Dircksenstraße.

While we're here, the giant *Fernsehturm* is worth a visit for the views if not the food. It's also worth a laugh, because once it was finished, it was realized that the sun shining on the windows of the ball at the top created a shimmering cross. Built in 1969, the atheist, communist regime was suddenly stuck with a symbol they didn't want and the populace responded by calling the tower "the Pope's Revenge" or *Die Rache des Papstes*. Every trick was attempted to eliminate the reflection but all failed. Another popular name for the 220 meter tall structure is the *"Telespargel"* or TV Asparagus. Known as *"Fernmeldeturm 32"*[98] in the construction blueprints, the tower was used as a surveillance post by the MfS Stasi to keep tabs on its citizens who must have appeared as worker ants in the streets so far below.

The Friedrichstraße Train Station and Weidendammer Brücke — both featured in "The Bourne Supremacy" — are also nearby. In the movie, Bourne makes his escape from by leaping onto a boat from the Bridge over the Spree.

---

[98] Trans: Telecommunications tower.

World Time Clock — 2024 (credit: author)

Welt Zeit Uhr — 1972 (BA Bild_183-L0328-0016)

Weidendammer Brücke (credit: author)

TV Tower & Bode Museum from Weidendammer Brücke
(credit: author)

Oberbaumbrücke

First built in 1724 as a wooden drawbridge, the Oberbaum Bridge links Friedrichshain and Kreuzberg, which were formerly divided by the Berlin Wall, and has become an important symbol of Berlin's unity. It was rebuilt in the late 1800s as a stone arch bridge with the distinctive towers. Looking south from the bridge along the river, this was the main axis of the Russian advance into the city in 1945. Heavily damaged in that battle, it was repaired after the war. During the Cold War, it was an important crossing point open to pedestrians from East to West.

The lower deck of the bridge is a roadway while the upper deck carries U-Bahn lines U1 and U3, between Schlesisches Tor and Warschauer Straße stations.

The bridge appeared in the films *Run Lola run, Unknown, the Bourne Supremacy,* and *Berlin Station.* The nearby U-Bahn Station Schlesisches Tor also appeared in the movie *The Quiller Memorandum* (1966).

— Oberbaumbrücke, U-Bahnhof Schlesisches Tor (U1, U3)

Oberbaumbrücke from the Southeast (credit: author)

The most beautiful bridge in Berlin - Oberbaumbrücke (credit: author)

Messedamm Underground — A cinematic star that looks nicer in the movies.

In the northwestern part of the city, the underground tunnel at the *Messe Berlin* (exhibition grounds) in Charlottenburg-Wilmersdorf has been filmed on numerous occasions including the movies *The Atomic Blonde, Bourne Supremacy, Mockingjay - Part 2, Hanna,* and *Captain America: Civil War,* while *The Quiller Memorandum* was filmed on the streets above.

Situated beneath the streets near the International Congress Center and the famous *Funkturm* (Radio Tower). The tower was built by Heinrich Straumer and opened on September 3, 1926. As a transmission mast, it is now only used for police radio. There are good views of the city from the Funkturm restaurant and its observation deck.

— *Messegelände Berlin,* Masurenallee and Messedamm opposite the Haus des Rundfunks
S-Bahnhof Messe Nord ICC (Witzleben) S41, S42

The Messegelände underground looks better in the Movies (credit: author)

Messegelände & Funkturm (Conference Center & Radio Tower) (credit: author)

Hotel Adlon

Located on the famous Pariser Platz and very close to the Brandenburg Gate, the Hotel Adlon first opened on October 23, 1907. The Kaiser and many other notables attended the opening and it quickly became the social center of Berlin. During the 1920s, the Adlon was one of the most famous hotels in Europe and hosted many notables.

The main building was mostly destroyed by a fire after WWII had ended and for most of the Cold War only a small annex was used by guests. Around 1970, the East German government renovated the annex to use as a lodging house for government apprentices. In 1984, what remained of the hotel was demolished. After reunification in 1990, the land was acquired by the Keminski Group and a "new" Adlon was opened in 1997, 90 years after the opening of the first.

The hotel has featured in numerous fiction and non-fiction books, including Joseph Kanon's *The Good German,* as well as the Bernie Gunther novels by Philip Kerr, and William L. Shirer's memoir *Berlin Diary.* Much of the Liam Neeson 2011 action film "Unknown" was filmed at the Adlon. Notable guests have included Michael Jackson (and son), as well as the cast of the James Bond film "Spectre" which premiered in the city in 2015, but it wasn't filmed there.

Hotel Adlon, Unter den Linden 77

007 in Adlon Library (credit: author & Photoshop)

Treadstone Encounter Haus — *The Bourne Supremacy*

"We're the last two."— Jarda to Bourne

A private home tucked away in a quiet upscale neighborhood was the scene of a violent confrontation between Jason Bourne and another Treadstone assassin, a man called Jarda who thought Bourne had lost his memory. Apparently, Bourne did forget everything excepy where Jarda lived. Bourne needs answers but doesn't really get them and the scene ends with a spectacular explosion.

In the movie *Bourne Supremacy,* we're led to believe this takes place in Munich, but it didn't. The scene was filmed in the Grossen Wannsee area of southwestern Berlin.

— Haus at 35 Kaiserstrasse, Wannsee

The Bourne Supremacy Confrontation Haus (credit: author)

The "Bridge of Spies" opened 18 hours later than the other checkpoints. (credit: author)

Glienicker Brücke — Bridge of Spies

The bridge as a venue for prisoner exchanges has appeared frequently in fiction. It appeared in the 1966 film, *Funeral in Berlin,* based on the novel by Len Deighton.[99] The 2015 Steven Spielberg film, *Bridge of Spies*, starring Tom Hanks and Sir David Mark Rylance, features the Powers–Abel prisoner exchange on the actual bridge.

— Glienicke Bridge, Königstraße / Berliner Straße 77–81, S-Bahn (S7) to Potsdam Hauptbahnhof, then via Tram (93) or Bus (N16) to Schloss Glienicke.

---

[99] This scene was actually filmed at the Swinemünder Brücke near the Gesundbrunnen S-Bahnhof.

CHAPTER XIV
Nearly finished, some "Tourist" Places...

What follows are some "not strictly" Cold War sites. They are places well worth visiting because they add context to the history of Berlin and the Cold War. Each in its own way contributed to the war by playing a part in Nazi Germany's Third Reich. Even the *Neue Wache,* which began life in the 19th Century as a guard house and then became a memorial to fallen soldiers became an important political symbol to the Nazis and successive regimes.

Reichstag

Berlin's Reichstag was the meeting place of the German Empire's legislature and later that of the Weimar Republic. Finished in 1884, its most controversial moment came when it was burned in a fire allegedly set by a communist on 27 February 1933, precisely four weeks after Adolf Hitler had been sworn in as Chancellor of Germany. Hitler used the fire as a pretext for cracking down on communists by suspending civil liberties, and pursued the destruction of any political opposition by pushing President Paul von Hindenburg to issue the oppressive "Decree for the Protection of People and State." During WWII, the building stood empty for the most of the war. After the armistice and under the 1971 Four Power Agreement on Berlin, the Reichstag was not used because Berlin was theoretically restricted from any governmental affairs of either East or West Germany.[100] It stood mostly as a hopeful symbol for an eventual reunification and a sometime canvas for art, such as Christo's "Wrapped Reichstag" in 1995. On 3 October 1990, the building became again the seat of the German parliament.

    — Reichstag, Platz der Republik, U-Bahnhof (Station) Brandenburger Tor, (U5, S1, S2, S25, or S26)

---

[100] This agreement was ignored by the East Germans who made Berlin (East) their capital, while West Germany located its capital in Bonn until it returned to a united Berlin in 1991.

Soviet soldiers raising flag over Reichstag 1945 (PD)

Reichstag 2024 (credit: author)

Reichstag from West at Night 2014 (credit:Ansgar Koreng / CC BY-SA 3.0 (DE)

Reichstag Wrapped by Christo 1995 (credit: author)

NVA soldier with torch inside Neue Wache 1970 (credit: BA Bild 183-J0930-0035-001, Peter Koard / CC BY-SA 3.0)

NVA Guard Regiment Soldier at the Neue Wache 1978 (credit: author)

Neue Wache

The work of architect Karl Friedrich Schinkel who designed many Neoclassical and neo-Gothic buildings, the *Neue Wache* (New Watch) has gone through four transformations since it was first built as a guard house for the soldiers near the palace of King Friedrich Wilhelm III in 1818. After WWI and the end of the Prussian monarchy it was turned into a "Memorial for the Fallen of the War" by the Weimar Republic. It remained largely in this configuration (with the addition of a wooden cross by the Nazis) through the era of the Third Reich and the occupation of East Berlin by the USSR. In 1960, the German Democratic Republic changed it to a "Memorial to the Victims of Fascism and Militarism." An eternal flame was placed in the center of the hall inside of a glass cube in 1969 and the remains of an unknown soldier along with those of an unknown resistance fighter were placed in an underground chamber.

Although it had been guarded by German soldiers from the Prussian empire, the Third Reich, to the *NVA-Wachregiment* (guard regiment), following the fall of the Berlin Wall and the reunification of Germany, Chancellor Helmut Kohl announced that the *Neue Wache* would become transformed into a "Central Memorial of the Federal Republic of Germany for the Victims of War and Tyranny."

Featured in the courtyard of the building is an enlarged replica of Käthe Kollwitz's 1937 sculpture "Mother with her Dead Son," a modern Pieta. The statue was installed after reunification in 1993.[101] Although there were many debates about the inclusion of such Christian iconography, Kohl was insistent that the symbol be included signifying the unity of Germany.

— The *Neue Wache* is located at Unter den Linden 4, U-Bahnhof (Station) Museumsinsel (U5)

---

[101] Harald Haacke created an enlarged copy of Kollwitz's original sculpture for the memorial.

Neue Wache 2024
(credit: author)

Statue "Mother with
her Dead Son" after
Katje Kollwitz 2024
(credit: author)

Dom Cathedral in profile, 1990 (credit: author)   Dom Cathedral in profile, 2024 (credit: author)

Dom — Berlin Cathedral

Part of the beautiful history of Berlin, but in an empirical way,[102] as The Berliner Dom has no real part in espionage or, for that matter, the Cold War. I have included it because the cathedral is referred to as the Protestant rival of St. Peter's Basilica in Rome and is one of the most impressive buildings and locations in the city.

Built for the Hohenzollern dynasty and completed in 1905, the Dom is the seat of the Protestant Supreme Parish and Collegiate Church and tomb for the Hohenzollern emperors and family. Much of the church was damaged in WWII and parts were demolished by the East German government. Its restoration began in 1975, partly because of the influx of West Marks from the Protestant Church in West Germany (with strict controls on the religious symbolism reinstalled in the church). After reunification, a full rebuild of the cathedral began, including the massive pipe organ built by Wilhelm Sauer.

— Berliner Dom, Museum Island, U-Bahnhof (station) Museumsinsel, (U5, U2, U8), U-Bahnhof Alexanderplatz (S3, S5, S7, S9, S75), Tram Stop: Spandauer Straße (M4, M5, M6), Bus Stop: Am Lustgarten (100, 200, 300)

---

102 Pun intended.

Brandenburg Gate

While the Reichstag stood as the hopeful symbol of Germany's reunification, the *Brandenburger Tor* was the probably the most recognizable symbol of its division. Once the Wall fell, the Gate became the overarching symbol of a reunified Germany.

It is the only surviving city gate in Berlin, built between 1788 and 1791, and is the city's first Greek revival building, designed by Carl Gotthard Langhans. It is topped with the Quadriga statue, which was once stolen and carted off to Paris by Napoleon when he captured the city in 1806. When Napoleon was booted out of power (he abdicated) in 1814 following the occupation of Paris by the Sixth Coalition, it was returned to Berlin by Field Marshal Gebhard von Blücher.

When the Wall was built, the Brandenburg Gate fell just inside the Soviet sector's exclusion zone and was inaccessible for anyone beside East Germany's Frontier Troops (Grenztruppen) until the Wall fell and the Gate was reopened on 22 December 1989.

The statue known as the "Quadriga," originally named the "Procession of Peace" by the sculptor, Johann Gottfried Schadow, represents the four-horse chariot of the gods, driven by Victoria, the Roman the Goddess of Victory, "who brings peace." It was placed atop the gate in 1793.

The gate was not spared the destruction of the Second World War. Luckily, a pre-war original protective clay mold of the Quadriga was discovered that allowed a reconstructed statue to be placed back

Brandenburg Gate, 1962 (credit: Jim Wilde)

Brandenburg Gate, 1977 (credit: author)

Brandenburg Gate, 1992 (credit: author)

Brandenburg Gate Quadriga, 2024 (credit: author)

on the gate in 1958, as it had always been, facing East. Because of the sensitivities of the East German authorities, a Maltese Cross, which had been originally incorporated inside the olive wreath on Victoria's staff, was left off the reconstructed statue.[103] The cross was only returned to its place after reunification.

Pariser Platz is also home to two prominent embassies: France and the United States. Both had their Chancery buildings here prior to WWII and both were destroyed in the final fight for the city (the Palais Beauvryé and Palais Blücher respectively).

— Brandenburg Gate, U-Bahnhof Brandenburger Tor (U5, S1, S2, S25, or S26)

---

[103] An interesting point as the East German military adopted many of the traditions of its forerunner, the *Wehrmacht*.

Victory Column, 2024
(credit: author)

Siegessäule - celebrating the first German Unification

In the heart of Tiergarten Park, the *Siegessäule* (Victory Column) with its golden statue is one of the city's must-see sights. From the Brandenburg Gate, the *Straße des 17. Juni* leads west through the centre of Tiergarten Park. If you stroll down it for around twenty minutes, you reach a major intersection – a vast traffic circle called the *Großer Stern*. In its center you will see the Victory Column.

Work began in 1864. Designed by Heinrich Strack, the column was initially intended to celebrate Prussia's victory in the war against Denmark. By the time the column was finished in 1873, Prussia was also celebrating two more victories in the Austro-Prussian War and the Franco-Prussian War. The Kingdom of Prussia had successfully united Germany as an imperial power under the Prussian crown and these wars became known as The Wars of German Unification.

A column of three segments topped with a bronze sculpture with reliefs and a mosaic frieze recount the story of founding the German Empire. It was first installed on Königsplatz square in front of the Reichstag Parliament building, but was moved to its present location in 1938 as part of Hitler's plan to transform Berlin into a world capital called *"Germania."* When it was moved, a fourth section was added, raising the column to a height of 67 meters.

The monument made it through the Second World War largely unscathed. The Soviet / Russian soldiers who occupied the capital used her position to navigate the city and called her the "Golden Lady."

Victory, 2024
(credit: author)

Sitting on a base of Swedish red granite, the base contains four bronze reliefs depicting scenes from the three victories designed by Moritz Schulz, Karl Keil, Alexander Calandrelli, and Albert Wolff. A round hall on the base is decorated with a glass mosaic designed by Anton von Werner.

Above the hall are four sandstone columns, the first three containing 20 gilded gun barrels each, from bottom to top: Danish 12-pounders, Austrian 8-pounders, and French 4-pounders from each victory.

On top sits the 8.5 meter gilded bronze victory which weighs 35 tons.[104] She represents Victoria, the Roman goddess of victory. She holds a laurel wreath in one hand and, in the other, a spear decorated with an iron cross set in a wreath. Her helmet is adorned by an eagle, which symbolizes Borussia, the personification of Prussia. Locally, she is known as *"Goldelse,"* or "Golden Elsie."

— Siegessäule, Großer Stern, S-Bahnhof Tiergarten (S3, S5, S7, S9)

---

104 Alings, Reinhard. *Die Berliner Siegessaule: Vom Geschichtsbild zum Bild der Geschichte.* Berlin: Parthas Verlag GmbH, 2000.

Kaiser-Wilhelm Gedächtniskirche

Step inside the Kaiser-Wilhelm Memorial Church from the chaos of the nearby Kurfürstendamm and suddenly the hectic world is gone. This is one of Berlin's most important churches and, at the same, a memorial for peace and reconciliation as it commemorates Berliners' determination to rebuild after the war. A landmark in the divided city known as the "Hollow Tooth," it was rebuilt from the ruins of the original that was destroyed in World War II and includes a modern church building, a place of contemplation.

Constructed between between 1891 and 1895, it was built in honor of Wilhelm I, the first German Kaiser, by his grandson Wilhelm II by (???) Franz Schwechten in the Neo-Romantic style.

With five spires, its design reflected the tastes of the time. Its five bellswere the second biggest in Germany after Cologne and when the church was inaugurated, the bells rang so loudly that the wolves in the nearby Zoo started howling.

During the Second World War, they were silenced and removed to be melted down for munitions. Air raids damaged the church in 1943; the top of the main spire broke off and the roof partially collapsed. Following the war, the ruin stood as a reminder of the horrors of war.

In 1956, the city planned to demolish the church and build a new one but a compromise was reached to integrate the ruins into the design for the new church. The architect Egon Eiermann directed the project and it was completed in 1961. The design includes a memorial hall in the old spire, a symbol against war and of reconciliation

Inside the nave, the rich blue stained glass produces an atmosphere of meditative calm. It also contains a crucifix made of nails from the burnt roof timbers of Coventry Cathedral, which was almost completely destroyed by German bombs in 1940. The cross is a symbol of reconciliation.

— Kaiser-Wilhelm Gedächtniskirche, Breitscheidplatz, Bahnhof Zoo (S3), Wittenbergplatz U-Bahnhof (U1, U2, U3)

Kaiser-Wilhelm Gedächtniskirche looking East from the Ku'damm, 1977 (credit: author)

Kaiser-Wilhelm Gedächtniskirche looking East from tthe Ku'damm, 2024 (credit: author)

Chapel Blue Christ, 2024 (credit: author)

Museumsinsel Berlin — the cultural and artistic center of the city

Situated in the middle of the Spree River with its classical and modern buildings and magnificent collections of art, Berlin's Museum Island is hard to miss and one of its most beautiful locations. It was also recognized by UNESCO as a World Cultural Heritage site in 1999.

The plan for Museum Island was driven by the humanistic ideals of the Enlightenment that prevailed in the early 19th century. Leading German architects of the day, Karl Friedrich Schinkel and Friedrich August Stüler, shaped the development of the island, Berlin's birthplace and its current urban heart. Their Neo-classical architecture was introduced to the public with the opening of the Königliches Museum, now known as the Altes Museum, in 1830 under the reign of Friedrich Wilhelm IV. It marked the Museumsinsel Berlin as a "sanctuary of art and science." It was followed by the Neues Museum (1843–1855), the Nationalgalerie (1867–1876), the Bode-Museum (1897–1904), first known as the Kaiser Friedrich-Museum, and finally the Pergamonmuseum (1910–1930). The New Museum is now home to the famous bust of Egyptian Queen Nefertiti, which was formerly displayed at Charlottenburg Palace.

During the Second World War, collections belonging to the state of Prussia were dispersed over the country and many pieces were lost. The buildings were severely damaged in the final Battle of Berlin.

After 1990 and with the reunification of Germany, the collections of former East and West Berlin were merged, and the museum buildings were renovated. Now Berlin's Museum Island stands as a testament to the City's preservation of 6,000 years of history and its commitment to the study and presentation of civilization.

— Museum Island, Bodestrasse 1-3, U-Bahnhof Museumsinsel (U5), S-Bahnhof Alexanderplatz (S3)

Museum Island Colonnade Courtyard with view of TV Tower & the Pope's Revenge, 2024 (credit: author)

Alte Nationalgalerie, 2024 (credit: author)

The Wannsee House and the Final Solution

On January 20, 1942, a 90-minute meeting at a villa located on the idyllic Grossen Wannsee sealed the fate of six million Jewish citizens of Europe.

Fifteen men discussed and agreed upon the logistics and responsibilities of a plan called the *Endlösung der Judenfrage (The Final Solution of the Jewish Question)* which had already been devised and ordered into effect by Germany's *Führer* Adolf Hitler.

Those fifteen men set the plan set in motion. They were:

- SS General Reinhard Heydrich, the chief of the Reich Security Main Office
- SS Major General Heinrich Müller, chief of RSHA Department IV (Gestapo)
- SS Lieutenant Colonel Adolf Eichmann, Chief, RSHA Department IV B 4 (Jewish Affairs)
- SS Colonel Eberhard Schöngarth, commander of the RSHA field office in Krakow, Poland
- SS Major Rudolf Lange, commander of RSHA Einsatzkommando 2
- SS Major General Otto Hofmann, the chief of SS Race and Settlement Main Office.
- State Secretary Roland Freisler (Ministry of Justice)
- Ministerial Director Wilhelm Kritzinger (Reich Cabinet)
- State Secretary Alfred Meyer (Reich Ministry for the Occupied Eastern Territories - USSR)
- Ministerial Director Georg Leibrandt (Reich Ministry for the Occupied Eastern Territories)
- Undersecretary of State Martin Luther (Foreign Office)
- State Secretary Wilhelm Stuckart (Ministry of the Interior)
- State Secretary Erich Naumann (Office of Plenipotentiary for the Four-Year Plan)
- State Secretary Josef Bühler (Office of the Governor General-German-occupied Poland)
- Ministerial Director Gerhard Klopfer (Nazi Party Chancellery)

On 31 July 1941, Hermann Göring gave written instructions to prepare and submit a plan for the "final solution" in territories under German control. The "Final Solution" was the code name for the deliberate, carefully planned destruction, or elimination, of all European Jews. That vague term was meant to hide a policy of mass murder from the rest of the world. In fact, the men at Wannsee talked about methods of killing, about liquidation, about "extermination."

The Wannsee Conference, as it became known to history, did not mark the beginning of the "Final Solution." Mobile squads called *Einsatzgruppen* were already slaughtering Jews in the occupied Soviet Union.

The Wannsee Conference was to formally reveal the plan to non-Nazi leaders who would arrange for Jews to be transported from all over German-occupied Europe to SS-operated Konzentrationslager or Concentration Camps in occupied Poland. None of the men present objected to a policy that for the first time committed a nation-state to the murder of an entire people.

The plan's intent was ominously clear:

"Under proper guidance, in the course of the final solution the Jews are to be allocated for appropriate labor in the East. Able-bodied Jews, separated according to sex, will be taken in large work columns to these areas for work on roads, in the course of which action doubtless a large portion will be eliminated by natural causes. The possible final remnant will, since it will undoubtedly consist of

Wannsee Haus (credit: A.Savin, Wikipedia)

the most resistant portion, have to be treated accordingly, because it is the product of natural selection and would, if released, act as the seed of a new Jewish revival."[105]

The villa still stands and serves as a memorial and education center and chilling reminder of the Holocaust. There is permanent exhibition entitled The Wannsee Konferenz and the Extermination of European Jewry, and includes a reconstruction of the room where the discussions took place. Also shown are the minutes of the conference taken by Adolf Eichmann and the photographs of the civil servants and SS officers involved. A chronicle of the events and the horrors surrounding the Holocaust from the deportations to the exterminations in the concentration camps comprises the rest of the exhibit.

— Haus der Wannsee-Konferenz, Haus am Grossen Wannsee 56-58

---

[105] John Mendelsohn, ed., The Holocaust: Selected Documents in Eighteen Volumes. Vol. 11: The Wannsee Protocol and a 1944 Report on Auschwitz by the Office of Strategic Services (New York: Garland, 1982), 18-32.

Gestapo
Headquarters Prinz
Albrecht Straße 8
(credit: PD)

Topography of Terror — *Gestapo* Headquarters

The *Gestapo* or Secret State Police was one of two Nazi security agencies that were totally above the law.[106] Heinrich Müller led the organization and was answerable to Heinrich Himmler, the head of the SS or *Schutzstaffel* (Protection Squadron). Once Hitler came to power, the function of the *Gestapo* was simply to ensure no one would challenge the dominance of the Nazi Party and its leadership. Effectively the Gestapo was following what was known as the *Nacht und Nebel* (Night and Fog) Decree, which stated:

"Efficient and enduring intimidation can only be achieved either by capital punishment or by measures by which the relatives of the criminals do not know the fate of the criminal."[107]

The *Gestapo* was the primary action arm of the Nazi's political police system and was responsible for much of the terror of *Kristallnacht* (Night of Broken Glass), which terrorized the Jewish population, its businesses, and destroyed its places of worship. The Final Solution and the Holocaust that followed were largely orchestrated by both the Gestapo and the SS.

What remains of the building's basement and former holding cells was only excavated in the 1980s and first displayed in conjunction with Berlin's 750th Anniversary in 1987. The *Topographie des Terrors* (Topography of Terror) is an outdoor and indoor history museum on Niederkirchnerstrasse, formerly named Prinz-Albrecht-Strasse, near the Brandenburg Gate and Checkpoint Charlie.

— *Topographie des Terrors,* Niederkirchnerstraße 8, U-bahnhof Brandenburger Tor (U5, S1, S2, S25, or S26)

---

[106] The other agency was the SS *Sicherheitsdienst* (Security Service) or SD led by Reinhard Heydrich until he was assassinated in Prague.

[107] After receiving the verbal decree from Hitler on 7 December, 194, *Generalfeldmarschall* Wilhelm Keitel explained them in written orders to the security organizations. Many of these same methods were later used by the *Stasi.*

Kristallnacht
Memorial, 2024
(credit: author)

Berlin Wall Remnant
& Topography of
Terror Museum,
2024 (credit: author)

The Bendler Block and *"Unternehmen Walküre"*

The new home of the German Ministry of Defense, the Bendler Block, was the headquarters of the Nazi German *Oberkommando der Wehrmacht* (Armed Forces High Command) during World War II and the scene where the final attempted assassination of Adolf Hitler was planned out, a plan called Operation Valkyrie *(Unternehmen Walküre).*

On July 20, 1944, Colonel Claus Schenk Graf von Stauffenberg and a few confidants tried in vain to bring about the overthrow of the Nazi regime from this location and at Adolf Hitler's *Wolfsschanze* (Wolf's Lair) headquarters in Rastenburg, East Prussia (today Poland). When their plot failed, he and his closest confidants were executed by firing squad in the inner courtyard of the Bendlerblock that same night.

The plan began months earlier, when several senior German Army (*Heer*) officers — all members of the *Oberkommando des Herres* (Supreme High Command of the Army) — decided to remove Hitler from power. They had lost hope that Germany could win the war and blamed Hitler for leading Germany to disaster. Secretly, some politicians and senior military officials began to plan Hitler's assassination.

The planners used an existing emergency continuity-of-government operations plan, called *Unternehmen Walküre* or Operation Valkyrie, intended to be implemented in the event of a general breakdown in national civil order due to Allied bombing of German cities, a reserve army of the *Wehrmacht* was to protect the government and put down the uprising. The plan was adopted by Stauffenberg's group and adapted to their goals.

General Friedrich Olbricht, Major General Henning von Tresckow and Colonel Claus von Stauffenberg modified the plan with the intention of using it to take control of German cities, disarm the SS, and arrest the Nazi leadership once Hitler had been assassinated in the 20 July plot. Hitler's death was deemed necessary to free German soldiers from their oath of loyalty to him.

Key to the plan was gaining access to Hitler in order to place a small explosive device in a briefcase close enough to kill him when it exploded. Colonel Stauffenberg was chosen to carry the bomb into the Wolf's Lair because of his status on the German General Staff and reputation as a wounded war hero.

On July 20, 1944, Stauffenberg arrived at Wolfsschanze. The conspirators thought the meeting would happen as usual in the main underground bunker. Had it happened there, the blast would have killed everyone in the room, however, it was an extremely hot day and the meeting was moved to the above ground bunker, which had greater air circulation. The room had numerous windows meaning the explosion would be significantly reduced as the energy of the blast would be dissipated.

Stauffenberg understood this but continued with the operation, believing the bomb would be adequate. Before the meeting, Stauffenberg went to a private room ostensibly to change his shirt but in reality to arm the two 1-kilo explosive devices in the briefcase. He was interrupted by a phone call and an aide pounding on the door, which meant he could only arm one device.

Thus handicapped, Stauffenberg knew he had to place the briefcase as close to Hitler as possible in order to do any sort of damage. He was able to secure a seat as close to Hitler as possible, and put the briefcase as close to Hitler as he could. A co-conspirator arranged to call Stauffenberg on the telephone so he could leave the room.

After he left, another officer moved into Stauffenberg's place and moved the briefcase, placing it on the other side of a heavy wooden table away from Hitler's position thus protecting *Der Führer* when the bomb went off. One person was killed immediately, three died later, and twenty others were wounded including Hitler.

Believing Hitler was dead, Stauffenberg rushed back to Berlin by airplane where the other conspirators were gathered in preparation to putting Operation Valkyrie into effect.

When it became clear that Hitler had survived, Valkyrie withered. Some of plotters committed suicide while others were arrested, tortured and executed. Betrayed by one of his co-plotters, Stauffenberg was executed that night, though not before shouting "Long live holy Germany" as he faced down the firing squad in the Bendler Block. A total of around 200 conspirators were executed in the following weeks and months.

While their actions were laudable — the plotters wanted to end the war — they were by no means "angels of innocence." Many had supported Hitler and some were guilty of war crimes. Their motivation was a simple calculus: they knew the war was lost and wanted to save the homeland from complete destruction.

A memorial was unveiled in the inner courtyard of the Bendlerblock on July 20, 1953, creating a place of remembrance and commemoration for all members of the resistance movement against Hitler and the National Socialist Party.

— *die Gedenkstätte Deutscher Widerstand,* Stauffenbergstraße 13 - 14 (formerly Bendlerstraße),

Bus Stop Gedenkstätte Deutscher Widerstand (M 29), Bahnhof Kurfürstenstraße (U1), Bahnhof Potsdamer Platz (U2, S1, S2, S25, S26).

Bendler Block Memorial Plaque, 2024
(credit: author)

Silent Hero Statue, designed by Professor Richard Scheibe, 2024
(credit: author)

Site of Hitler's
Bunker, 2024
(credit: author)

Hitler's Bunker — *Das dicke Ende kommt noch*[108]

It is fitting to end our short tour of pre-Cold War "tourist sites" with a visit to Hitler's Bunker, although "nothing to see here" might be the proper name for this site. What remains is an empty parking lot that marks the location of Adolf Hitler's Chancery and headquarters during World War II. Part of the complex included the *Führerbunker* (Leader's Bunker), built deep under the Chancery garden to protect the Nazi leadership during Allied air raids and the final Russian ground assault on Berlin in May 1945.

On 30 April 1945, Hitler finally accepted that his Thousand Year Reich was only going to last twelve years and committed suicide by shooting himself deep inside the bunker. His body was found with that of his long-time mistress Eva Braun, who married Hitler only hours before and committed suicide with him. Reportedly, they were burned in a shell crater in the garden by his aides. Unless, of course, he escaped to Brazil with Martin Bormann.

Unlike the memorials to the victims of National Socialism, the German government rightly does nothing to celebrate the perpetrators – or chief perpetrator, Adolf Hitler, and his legacy.

Not much to look at or experience here. There is only an information board on the site. More appropriately, the Holocaust Memorial and the *Topographie des Terrors* are nearby. There are also several good restaurants in the area, as well as Checkpoint Charlie and its museum.

— The *Führerbunker*, Corner of Gertrud-Kolmar-Straße & in der Ministergarten, U-bahnhof Brandenburger Tor (U5, S1, S2, S25, or S26)

Deutsches Spionagemuseum / German Spy Museum Berlin

Opened in 2015, the German Spy Museum is an idea of journalist Franz-Michael Günther devoted to the history of spies and espionage in the former spy capital. It's exhibits cover far more than spy games in Berlin and delve deeply into the history of espionage from Biblical times to the present day with historical items and high-tech multimedia installations.

— Leipziger Platz 9, 10117 Berlin.

---

[108] The worst is yet to come.

CHAPTER XV
The Cold War Ended, Didn't It?

It All Falls Down.

When the Wall fell, the world expected an end to the superpower conflict between the Warsaw Pact and NATO that dragged on for so long. A brief hiatus ensued and it seemed that peace might indeed take hold. But, as is so often the case in human history, that brief pause was soon superseded by new ambitions and a seeming resolve by a new Russian government to re-establish itself as the worthy successor to the Czar and Imperial Russia.

The Wall Falls — Nov 10, 1989 (credit: author)

From the same vantage point - a "wall" at Euro2024 (credit: author)

The End — West and East become Berlin once more (author's collection)

When the Wall collapsed on November 9, 1989, the government of the soon to be obsolete GDR decided to reform itself. A initial step was taken on March 2, 1990, when the GDR government passed a resolution to relieve all former unofficial employees of the Ministry for State Security (MfS) of their duties. This resolution was an important step in the political development of the GDR. It took into account the fears of the population that the former IMs could continue to engage in conspiratorial activities. It was also intended to protect the personal rights of the former IMs. Soon the MfS would be completely shut down. With the fall of the Berlin Wall along with the opening of frontiers between Eastern Europe and the West, the Soviet Union would also go through a massive upheaval, Within several years the Union of Soviet Socialist Republics would no longer exist, replaced by what the rest of the World hoped would be a kinder, gentler Russia. That dream would be soon dispelled.

Cold War animosity was not so easily forgotten. American, British and French troops planned their last military parade in Berlin on 18 June 1994 alone. When Russia asked to join with an honorary unit and an orchestra, this was denied. They said the date was too close to 17 June, the day on which day the Red Army had crushed the East German uprising in 1953. The Russians were also excluded from the farewell ceremony on 8 September 1994. They ended up staging their own a week earlier. On 31 August, thousands of their soldiers marched through Berlin singing in accented German, 'Germany, to you we reach out our hand as we return to our fatherland'. Chancellor Helmut Kohl looked on, but Russia marched alone. Hans Jung, an East German translator involved in the event, remembered that 'the Russians were not amused'.[109]

---

[109] Katja Hoyer, "The remarkable success of the Allied occupation of Germany," London: The Spectator (1828) Ltd, 8 September 2024.

Bruised Egos and Some Recent Events

A recognizably weaker but still dangerous Russia began to reassert itself and by the early 2000s, it seemed that a new Cold War has begun. The KGB would be replaced by the SVR but nothing in its personnel and operations really changed. One need only point to Russia's attempts to control the newly independent republics, its aggression in Crimea and Ukraine and its attempts to reassert itself in the Middle East and Africa, to realize that a new game is afoot.

The United States is also playing from a weaker hand while it tries to manage small wars and conflicts around the world with a foreign policy that avoids direct involvement. Its efforts have not been overly successful.

While NATO attempts to blunt Russia's actions in the Ukraine and protect the Baltic nations from attack, Russia itself is playing a long game with disinformation, provocations, murder, and industrial sabotage...all special military operations short of war; all meant to undermine the western coalition.

Russia's recent actions, most likely attributable to their intelligence services special purpose units like the GRU's Unit 29155 attest to their desire to weaken western resolve by chipping slowly away at vital services or to eliminate dissidents outside it borders or to sabotage logistical centers and factories that support Ukraine's defensive efforts. One need only look at several incidents that took place in Berlin to understand the Russian intent to intimidate its enemies.

In 2014, two ammunition warehouses in Vrbětice were destroyed in a sabotage operation by agents of Unit 29155. The ammunition was intended to be delivered to the Ukrainian army.

Vadim Krasikov, an SVR officer, shot and killed Zelimkhan Khangoshvili (alias Tornike Kavtarashvili) a Chechen dissident in Berlin's Kleiner Tiergarten park in August 2019. Krasikov was arrested in Berlin and convicted of murder. He was sentenced to life in prison but in 2024 he was exchanged for western prisoners held in Russia.

On 4 May 2024, a fire took place at the Diehl Metal Applications metallurgical plant located in the Lichterfelde area of Berlin. DMA manufactures the IRIS-T missiles being used in Ukraine.

There was a brief holiday from the old Cold War but it disappeared with the emergence of Vladimir Putin as Russia's de-facto President for life.

Russia is stepping up its efforts to silence, threaten and persecute opponents abroad. It is also behind much of the propaganda that is causing turmoil in political arenas around the world. Sabotage by "Little Green Men," political intrigue, and military actions by proxies or Russia's allies (Iran, North Korea) are beginning to fill the newspapers.

A new Cold War has begun and Berlin remains fully engaged in the Spy Game.

About The Author

James Stejskal spent thirty-five years as a "Green Beret" and CIA case officer living and conducting operations around the world during the Cold War and after 9/11. He has written five military history books, along with numerous articles, and received accolades for his book Masters of Mayhem: Lawrence of Arabia and the British Military Mission to the Hejaz. His fiction centers on intelligence and special operations and The Ratcatcher is the fifth book in his The Snake Eater Chronicles. He lives in northern Virginia with his wife, Wanda.

DOUBLE DAGGER

www.doubledagger.ca

Double Dagger Books is Canada's only military-focused publisher. Conflict and warfare have shaped human history since before we began to record it. The earliest stories that we know of, passed on as oral tradition, speak of war, and more importantly, the essential elements of the human condition that are revealed under its pressure.

We are dedicated to publishing material that, while rooted in conflict, transcend the idea of "war" as merely a genre. Fiction, non-fiction, and stuff that defies categorization, we want to read it all.

Because if you want peace, study war.

Acknowledgements

This guide would not have been possible without the assistance and help I received from many people and institutions. Foremost my publisher Phil Halton and his friend Vincent Iarocci who prompted me to take on the task. Florian Weiss & Dr. Jürgen Lillteicher of the Allied Museum Berlin assisted my research for images and history. Franziska Schultze and the staff at Berliner Unterwelten e.V (Berlin Underworld) helped find my way through the musty tunnels and provided some imagery.

I also want to thank the very knowledgable Jonathan Whitlam of Whitlam's Berlin Tours for his continuing on-line tour dialog and snagging me a photo of an U-Bahn Station I forgot to shoot on my last visit to the city. Rick Reinisch at Digital Recollections in Arlington, Virginia helped with perfect, if rushed scans of my old, dusty negatives — many of which appear herein. My old comrades with whom I served at various times in Berlin also came through with their provision of additional Cold War images. Simone Külow of the Bundesarchiv (Federal German Archive) was one of the most important assets I had for assembling this book. Her painstaking work digging up operational *Stasi* photos based on the vague descriptions I provided contributed greatly to the end product.

Of course, I would be remiss (and in deep trouble) if I didn't mention my wife and first editor. Thanks for putting up with me and my imagined deadlines.

Finally, I won't mention the people who can't be mentioned — my colleagues from various unnamed organizations who were with me in the shadows of Berlin and elsewhere around the world. **My special thanks go out to the authors and artists whose works I have quoted in this book. Your contributions to the story are what makes Berlin a special place. Thanks for being there.**

Resources

Valuable places to visit and enhance your experience:

Allierten Museum Berlin, Clayallee 135.

(https://www.alliiertenmuseum.de)

Bundesarchiv - Stasi-Unterlagen-Archiv (German Federal Archive - Stasi Records Archive)

(https://www.bundesarchiv.de/stasi-unterlagen-archiv/)

Berlin Wall Memorial

(https://www.stiftung-berliner-mauer.de/en/berlin-wall-memorial)

Berliner Unterwelten e.V., Brunnenstraße 105

Specialists in the study of Berlin's underground for the urban infrastructure – everything from utilities and transportation, to military command bunkers, and escape tunnels.

(Contact: https://www.berliner-unterwelten.de/en/index.html)

Museum Berlin-Karlshorst

Open-air exhibition in the museum garden on the history of the unconditional surrender of the Wehrmacht to the four victorious powers, the Soviet Union, the USA, Great Britain and France, on May 8, 1945 in Berlin-Karlshorst.

—Located at Zwieseler Straße 4, 10318 Berlin-Karlshorst

Whitlam's Berlin Tours

Specializing in custom in-depth (and entertaining) tours of Berlin in English and German.

Contact: www.whitlams-berlin-tours.com & jonny@whitlams-berlin-tours.com. Also: @whitlamsberlintours (IG) / @whitlamsberlin (X).

Deutsches Spionagemuseum / German Spy Museum Berlin

"a unique insight into the gloom of espionage right where the Wall once divided the city."

Leipziger Platz 9, 10117 Berlin

Biblio

Alings, Reinhard. *Die Berliner Siegessaule: Vom Geschichtsbild zum Bild der Geschichte.* Berlin: Parthas Verlag GmbH, 2000.

Appelius, Stefan, "Tod im Tränenpalast," article on-line: https://zeitschrift-fsed.fu-berlin.de, zdf 39/2016.

Bainbridge, John, "Die Mauer," *The New Yorker* magazine, October 19, 1962.

Bästlein, Klaus, *"Vom NS-Täter zum Opfer des Stalinismus: Dr. Walter Linse - Ein deutscher Jurist im 20. Jahrhundert,"* Schriftenreihe des Berliner Landesbeauftragten für die Unterlagen des Staatssicherheitsdienstes der ehemaligen DDR, Band 27, Berlin: BStU, 2008.

Beckner, Michael, *Muir's Gambit: A Spy Game Novel,* Montrose: Montrose Station Press, 2022.

Behling, Klaus, "Der Nachrichtendienst der NVA," Berlin: Edition Ost, 2005.

Berliner Mauer Gedenkstätte, "Czeslaw Jan Kukuczka" article on-line: http://www.berliner-mauer-gedenkstaette.de/en/1974-322,894,2.html.

Berry, I.S., *The Peacock and the Sparrow,* New York: Atria Books, 2024

Bilger, Burkhard, "The Stasi Files," The New Yorker, June 3, 2024. (Vol C, No 15), New York: Conde Nast, 2024.

Bundesarchiv-Stasi-Unterlagen-Archiv Berlin (BStU), *"Bautechnisches Gutachten über den Spionagetunnel in Altglienicke,"* Files: BStU, MfS, Abt. 26, Nr. 183, Bl. 28-36, retrieved 2023: https://www.stasi-mediathek.de/medien/bautechnisches-gutachten-ueber-den-spionagetunnel/blatt/28/

BStU, *"Fotoalbum vom Spionagetunnel in Altglienicke,"* Files: BStU, MfS, ZAIG, Fo, Nr. 2815, Bl. 2-26, retrieved 2023: https://www.stasi-mediathek.de/medien/fotoalbum-vom-spionagetunnel-in-altglienicke/

Charney, David L., M.D. and John A. Irvin, "The Psychology of Espionage," *The Intelligencer* - Journal of U.S. Intelligence Studies, Volume 22, Number 1, Falls Church: AFIO, Spring 2016.

CIA, "The Berlin Tunnel Operation: 1952 - 1956," Clandestine Service Historical Paper No. 150, Washington D.C., https://www.cia.gov/library/readingroom/docs/1968-06-24.pdf, retrieved 2024.

CIA, *Romeo Spies,* https://www.cia.gov/stories/story/romeo-spies/, article retrieved June 2018.

Deighton, Len, *Berlin Game,* London: Hutchinson & Co (Publishers) Ltd, 1986.

Engelberg, Stephen; Michael Wines, "U.S. Says Soldier Crippled Spy Post Set Up in Berlin," NY: *New York Times,* May 7, 1989.

Fricke, Karl Wilhelm, *"Vor 50 Jahren: Stasi-Aktion „Enten""*, Deutschlandradiofunk, (article on-line: https://www.deutschlandradio.de/unternehmen-106.html)

"G", "Engineering the Berlin Tunnel: Turning a Cold War Scheme into Reality," article in *Studies in Intelligence,* Vol. 52, No. 1 (Extracts-March 2008).

Gehlen, Reinhard, *The Service: The Memoirs of General Reinhard Gehlen,* Winter Park: World Publications, 1972

Herrington, COL Stuart A., *Traitors Among Us,* San Diego: Harcourt-Harvest, 1999.

Herron, Mick, *The Secret Hours,* London: Soho Crime, 2024.

Iken, Katja, Marc von Lüpke, "Ein Schuss, viele Fragen," *Der Spiegel*, Hamburg: SPIEGEL-Verlag, 18.02.2015.

Kanon, Joseph, *Leaving Berlin,* London: Simon & Schuster, 2014.

Kesaris, Paul. L, ed. *The Rote Kapelle: the CIA's history of Soviet intelligence and espionage networks in Western Europe,* 1936-1945, Washington DC: University Publications of America, 1979.

Kostka, Bernd von and Sven Felix Kellerhoff, *Capital of Spies,* Oxford: Casemate Publishers, 2021.

Kostka, Bernd von, "The Turkish Spy Handler: Hüseyin Yildirim," https://www.casemateuk.com/blog/2021/11/09/the-turkish-spy-handler-huseyin-yildirim/

Kundler, Prof. Herbert, "RIAS Berlin and the Americans," RIAS Berlin Kommission, 2024, (on-line article https://riasberlin.org/en/history/articles/)

Le Carré, John, *Smiley's People,* New York: Alfred A. Knopf, 1980.

Le Carré, John, The Spy Who Came In From The Cold, London: Victor Gollancz & Pan. 1963.

Magee, Aden C., The Cold War Wilderness of Mirrors: Counterintelligence and the U.S. and Soviet Military Liaison Missions 1947-1990, Casemate: Havertown, 2021.

Military History Branch, *USCOB/USAB Pam 870-1: Checkpoint Charlie,* Berlin: G-3 Division, Headquarters, US Command, Berlin and US Army, 1980.

Mendelsohn, John, ed., The Holocaust: Selected Documents in Eighteen Volumes. Vol. 11: The Wannsee Protocol and a 1944 Report on Auschwitz by the Office of Strategic Services, New York: Garland, 1982.

Mohler, James, "Spycraft and Soulcraft on the Front Lines of History: A Conversation with Former CIA Chief of Counterintelligence James Olson," retrieved from https://albertmohler.com/2021/04/28/james-olson/

Murphy, David E.; Kondrashev, Sergei A.; Bailey, George, Battle Ground Berlin, New Haven: Yale University Press, 1997.

Prados, John, ed., "The Secret War for Germany: CIA's Covert Role in Cold War Berlin Explored through Recently Declassified Documents," National Security Archive #792, Georgetown, 2022. retrieved from nsarchiv@gwu.edu.

Soch, Konstanze (Hg.), Gabriele Camphausen, *Stasi in Berlin: Die DDR-Geheimpolizei in der geteilten Stadt,* Berlin: BStU, 2022.

Stejskal, James, Special Forces Berlin: Clandestine Cold War Operations of the US Army's Elite, 1956–1990, Oxford: Casemate, 2017.

Urstadt, Bryant, "Cold Warrior," Hanover: Dartmouth Alumni Magazine, Jan/Feb 2008

Vidich, Paul, *The Matchmaker,* New York: Atria/Emily Bestler Books, 2016.

Weiser, Benjamin, *A Secret Life: The Polish Colonel, His Covert Mission, And The Price He Paid To Save His Country,* New York: PublicAffairs, 2004.

Wolfe, Markus, *The Man Without A Face,* New York: Times Books, 1997.

Wunschik, Tobias, *Die Hauptabteilung XXII: "Terrorabwehr" (MfS-Handbuch),* Berlin: BStU, 1996. http://www.nbn-resolving.org/urn:nbn:de:0292-97839421301414